ISBN-13: 978-1484189856 (paperback)

ISBN-10: 148418985X (paperback)

JUSTIFIED

MODERN REFORMATION

ESSAYS ON

THE DOCTRINE OF

JUSTIFICATION

SECOND EDITION

Edited by Ryan Glomsrud

and Michael S. Horton

*"He also told this parable to some who trusted
in themselves that they were righteous, and treated
others with contempt: 'Two men went up into
the temple to pray, one a Pharisee and the other
a tax collector.*

*The Pharisee, standing by himself, prayed thus:
'God, I thank you that I am not like other men,
extortioners, unjust, adulterers, or even like
this tax collector. I fast twice a week;
I give tithes of all that I get.'*

*But the tax collector, standing far off, would not even
lift up his eyes to heaven, but beat his breast, saying,
'God, be merciful to me, a sinner!'*

*I tell you, this man went down to his
house* justified, *rather than the other."*

(Luke 18:9–14)

TABLE OF CONTENTS

TABLE OF CONTENTS

TABLE OF CONTENTS

Modern Reformation is pleased to publish this second edition of classic essays on the doctrine of justification. We believe that the difference between law and grace, faith and works, and justification and sanctification lies at the heart of a true understanding of the gospel, the Christian life, and the renewal of Christ's church. The apostle Paul insists in his Epistle to the Romans that "to the one who does not work but trusts him who justifies the ungodly, his faith is counted as righteousness" (Rom. 4:5). The gospel comes to the undeserving by *grace alone* through *faith alone* in *Christ alone*. This fundamental conviction continues to divide Protestants and Roman Catholics, even in our day. Our deeds of kindness, our Christian obedience, and our personal virtues do not contribute to our justification before the living God; for as Paul argues, "if it is the adherents of the law who are to be the heirs, faith is null and the promise is void" (Rom. 4:13).

In this expanded volume we have added two classic essays under the heading "Union and Peace with Christ" in order to emphasize further the significance of justification for the Christian life, all in keeping with Paul's conclusion in Romans 5:1, "Therefore, since we have been justified by faith, we have peace with God through our Lord Jesus Christ." May all churches being reformed by the Word stand in the grace of Christ and "rejoice in hope of the glory of God."

Ryan Glomsrud
Executive Editor
Modern Reformation

Getting Perspective

BY RYAN GLOMSRUD

C ompared with the "Battle for the Bible," *sola fide* has not loomed large as a topic of conversation in evangelical circles in the past. The formal principle of the Reformation, *Scripture alone*, captured evangelical attention from the 1950s more than the material principle, *justification by faith alone*. And yet, one of the many flashpoints in evangelicalism in recent years has been between leading Baptist minister John Piper and Anglican Bishop N. T. Wright who are very much at odds, not on Scripture, but on the substance of biblical soteriology or the doctrine of salvation.

Wright has produced several volumes of biblical-theological work at the lay and academic level, many of which are controversial in their own right; but the rising public dispute began with Piper's *The Future of Justification: A Response to N. T. Wright* (Crossway, 2007) and continued with Wright's rejoinder, an elaboration of key Pauline teachings in *Justification: God's Plan & Paul's Vision* (IVP, 2009). Neither book pulls any punches and in places the side discussion is harsh: for Piper, biblical orthodoxy is at stake, and Wright returns fire by comparing critics such as Piper to flat-earthers, even Pharisees.[1]

Ironically, Wright and others are critical of overly "introspective" Protestants for having cast themselves in the role of "Paul" and the medieval church doctors as "Pharisees" at the time of the Reformation; yet Wright now has little trouble placing himself in the apostle's shoes against his "old perspective" agitators. "Someone in my position," he writes, "is bound to have a certain fellow-feeling with Paul in Galatia. He is, after all, under attack from his own right wing."[2] Within broader evangelicalism, however, the fever-pitch at which this debate is sometimes argued is not, one suspects, because of either Piper's or Wright's intense argumentation and escalating rhetoric, but because the topic is keenly felt to have been at issue well before the clash of these two evangelical leaders. In other words, the justification debate in evangelicalism actually goes back much earlier than the arrival of the New Perspective on Paul.

The five *"solas"* of the Reformation were at one time the consensus of Protestant-ism. Converging in the doctrine of justification, we are saved by grace alone (*sola gratia*) through faith alone (*sola fide*) because of Christ alone (*solus Christus*) all for God's glory alone (*soli Deo Gloria*), a message of good news that is revealed to us in Scripture alone (*sola scriptura*). Over the past number of years, unfor-tunately, evangelicals have been divided on these otherwise unifying truths, tending to associate what was once the lifeblood of the evangelical movement with merely "getting saved." While some evangelicals, including many teachers and high-profile pastors, have directly attacked the old Protestant consensus, undermining specifically the doctrine of justification, other rank-and-file believ-ers have simply come to believe that there should be a different emphasis in evangelical media on personal and social renewal, or on the *transformative* aspect of salvation—namely, sanctification—rather than the *declarative* aspect—God's justification of the ungodly. Being reckoned righteous in Christ is for many a mere preface to the central message of the need to become more Christ-like, a trend moving in the direction of spirituality and discipleship. And finally, there are self-identified evangelicals who have never even heard of the "*solas*" of the Reformation, much less the imputation of Christ's righteousness that is the crux of justification. Whether rejected outright, neglected, or simply unknown, it is evident that the gospel as traditionally understood has fallen on hard times.

Over the past thirty years debates over the doctrine of justification, though quieter than other controversies, have nonetheless been many and varied. There is no one history to which *Modern Reformation* can draw your attention. Suffice it to say, Wright, James Dunn, and E. P. Sanders (representative of the New Perspective on Paul) are not the cause of the present controversy. Rather, they represent at best a contemporaneous phenomenon that has in some ways galvanized evangelicals who were already conflicted over how to understand both the big-picture interpretation of the Bible, otherwise called biblical theology, as well as crucial exegetical details—in particular the scriptural teaching on law, justification, righteousness, faith, and the nature of God's interaction with his people in the time of Abraham and Moses. In the end, it matters little if we can pinpoint whether the slow rise of justification debates occurred before or at the same time as the New Perspective. The point is that similar debates have been playing out among Christian college Bible faculties, on evangelical seminary campuses, in some of the more purportedly "doctrinaire" denominations, and even at meetings (past and present) of the Evangelical Theological Society, mostly without reference to Wright or the disparate group of scholars working on Second Temple Judaism and the interpretation of the New Testament. It is therefore important to gain a proper perspective on our current situation. In these selections from *Modern Reformation*, a combination of new and classic articles, we want to present a few catalyzing arguments that have the potential to move forward what we think is a stalled debate in evangelicalism and the wider world of New Testament studies.

LEAVING DISPENSATIONALISM BEHIND

There is a great deal of complexity to the history of evangelical theology, more than can possibly be summed up in a brief introduction. Among the various factors we could call to mind, the emergence of *a post-dispensationalist evangelical academy* is one that is not typically acknowledged. Classic premillennial dispensationalism, as many will know, had a unique way of carving up the biblical narrative from Genesis to Revelation, and is still without question a very popular way of interpreting the Bible among laity. But with the flourishing of "neo-evangelical" institutions such as Christian colleges, seminaries, and publishing companies over the past thirty years, dispensationalism has slowly retreated from dominance among the teachers and scholars who labor to train the next generation of leaders. In its place, there has been an emphasis on the *unity of the biblical story*. This effort amounted to an attempt to flatten the contours of redemptive history and shave off the rough edges of the starkly delimited covenant "dispensations" known to previous generations. Without necessarily revising evangelical eschatology or end-times views, evangelicals now predominantly identify one story of "grace" from beginning to end. One is tempted to explain this shift in terms of "lumping" and "splitting," general categories that are sometimes helpful in getting one's bearings. For better or worse, the overcoming of dispensationalism's exegetical "splitting" or compartmentalizing of redemptive history into seven relatively discrete and non-overlapping covenants has given way to a new "lumping" mentality, or what some of the authors in this volume will refer to as "mono-" or "one-covenantalism," which essentially groups together God's successive redemptive acts into one large, reductionist covenant. Where the old dispensational consensus identified *difference* in a transition from *law to grace*, post-dispensational evangelicals recognize mostly (and sometimes exclusively) *unity* in a movement of uninterrupted *grace*.

In this evangelical shift, several crucial Reformation themes—some of which never sat very well with dispensationalists either—have become more and more controversial. If the accent in evangelical biblical theology is no longer on the contrast between works and grace, old and new, as understood by various Reformation Protestants, then traditional distinctions between law and gospel, faithfulness and faith, and Moses and Abraham have also fallen by the wayside. Because of the predominance of evangelical mono-covenantalism of various kinds, Reformation perspectives are now at the periphery of the most recent justification debate, and even defenders of justification neglect the full range of the early Protestant tradition's biblical-theological resources. Two general points are worth elaboration before introducing the contributions of this volume.

THE IN-HOUSE DEBATE

The current debate has every appearance of being centered on those scholars working from a post-dispensationalist set of presuppositions. In fact, one is tempted to construe the in-house evangelical debate over justification as a conflict between those who are working to hash out the details of this move to highlight the unity of the Bible.

Here one thinks especially of the legacy of Daniel P. Fuller, son of the cofounder of Fuller Seminary, former professor of the same from 1953 to 1993, and teacher of several generations of biblical scholars who now work at a variety of evangelical institutions. Others could be cited and influence is difficult to trace, but there is widespread agreement among Fuller's "students," loosely understood, on a number of key issues. 1) It is assumed that the Reformation distinction between *law and gospel* somehow smacks of older dispensationalism and therefore cannot (and should not) be reconciled with a post-dispensationalist narrative of "grace" and continuity. 2) It follows that the Reformation understanding of *grace* must surely have been slightly *antinomian* or insufficiently concerned with the need to obey the law or pursue sanctification and holy living; in other words, the Reformation is frequently caricatured as having relegated or pushed faithfulness and obedience to an obsolete "law" covenant, leaving a deficit in evangelical preaching of exhortations to keep the law. 3) Further, it is sometimes said that the Reformation understanding of *faith* was similarly one-sided in emphasis—in this case "intellectualist" or insufficiently personal because it allegedly did not include the renovation of moral behavior. These are simply part of the air that is breathed in our post-dispensationalist context, and in fact most of these claims were either stated explicitly or indirectly hinted at in two of Fuller's books: first his *Gospel and Law: Contrast or Continuum: The Hermeneutics of Dispensationalism and Covenant Theology,* and then the summation of his life's teaching in *The Unity of the Bible: Unfolding God's Plan for Humanity.*[3] Addressing the doctrine of justification, Fuller concluded that in light of his redrawing of the covenantal map and revision of these key issues, one should be ready to affirm that *"justification depends on persevering faith"* or faithfulness.[4] This view is now widespread in evangelicalism and shares much in common with Wright's interpretation of biblical teaching on salvation without having been learned from him directly.

The justification debate has not fallen along Arminian versus Calvinist lines, as it might have in the past, for many of Fuller's heirs are in fact restlessly "Calvinist." That is, they are drawn to the theme of God's sovereignty over all things and are eager to explain the doctrine of perseverance in grace-centered or even "Augustinian" terms. Many post-dispensationalist exegetes are neither Pelagian nor semi-Pelagian, but frequently engage in discussions about whether to self-identify as four-, five-, six-, or even seven-point Calvinists! In fact, there have even been those within properly Reformed denominations who have taken up this discussion, such as Norman Shepherd (formerly of Westminster Theological Seminary in Philadelphia). To the extent that Shepherd and other Reformed theologians attempted to integrate with evangelicalism and negotiate with older dispensationalist interpretations of the Bible, they made a corresponding attempt to weaken classic Reformed distinctions between the "covenant of works" and the "covenant of grace."

THE MISSING ELEMENT

Fortunately, many evangelicals have ably defended the doctrine of imputation, the great double exchange whereby our sins are reckoned to Christ on the cross and his righteousness is accounted to us that we might have life (2 Cor. 5:21). This double imputation is the very essence of the Protestant understanding of justification. However, not all imputational schemes have been set in the context of the Reformation tradition's fully developed biblical theology, a fact that owes much to the emergence of the mono-covenantalism I have been describing. What many post-dispensationalist theologians share in common, therefore, including the "Calvinists"—and in fact what Piper shares in common with Wright—is what they are missing, namely, an extended engagement with classic covenant theology. There are genuine exegetical insights available in this Reformation tradition, especially when it comes to negotiating continuity and discontinuity in the history of redemption. Going forward in a discussion sometimes requires looking back in order to discern what was missing at the outset. In our context today, we could benefit from returning to the tradition probably least thought of as holding any hope for the resolution of the justification debate: the Reformation tradition. And yet, that is the aim of this volume. In these pages we bring together Lutheran, Reformed, and Baptist theologians and biblical scholars who are able to unpack Reformational perspectives for thoughtful nonspecialists.

COVENANT AND JUSTIFICATION

To begin this volume, *Modern Reformation* editor-in chief and *White Horse Inn* radio co-host Michael Horton (re)introduces the basics of Reformed biblical theology so as to set justification in its proper and essential redemptive-historical context, thereby reinforcing the plausibility and importance of the Reformation "*solas*" for evangelical theology.[5] In chapter 1, Horton upsets the cart by engaging directly with both Wright and Piper on precisely the issues discussed thus far. While he deeply appreciates Piper's defense of imputation, Horton finds validity in several of Wright's criticisms of the lack of sweeping biblical theology, especially the diminutive importance of the Abrahamic covenant. Wright's rhetorically powerful description of the climax of the covenants and his vision of eschatological promise and fulfillment continue to be issues even for those who are otherwise sympathetic to Piper's defense of justification. Drawing from surprising sources, including Jewish scholar Jon D. Levenson and Pope Benedict XVI, Horton shows that a good deal of scholarship actually points away from mono-covenantalism—a point on which Piper and Wright would seem united, in contrast to the Reformed tradition—and toward a distinction between the Abrahamic and the Mosaic covenants.

Classic covenant theology is not a *via media*, or middle way, between two different kinds of mono-covenantalism, but a different theology entirely. Without sacrificing the grand redemptive-historical narrative, Horton uses covenant theology to address the relationship between the Old and New Testaments, as well as specific theological questions such as the relationships between faith and obedience, the legal and the relational, and law and gospel. Horton's constructive presentation offers an alternative perspective that Piper has not fully embraced and Wright has not sufficiently considered.[6]

LAW AND FAITH

A proper understanding of law and gospel is fundamental for a vigorous defense of the doctrine of justification because it builds these categories up from the history of the covenants revealed in Scripture. Nonetheless, there are multiple uses of the term *law* in both biblical and non-canonical writings. It is therefore important to clear up confusion about the law that sometimes occurs in evangelical (and Reformed) scholarship. This is a particular specialty of T. David Gordon, professor of religion and Greek at Grove City College, who further sets the stage in chapter 2. Through the law we come to know of our sinfulness in God's sight, as Horton explains in chapter 3, which is why Scripture teaches that justification is of the *ungodly* and not the righteous (Rom. 4:5).

It is difficult to overestimate the importance of the definition of *faith* in the ongoing evangelical debate. Is faith synonymous with faithfulness? Does faith have its potency or efficacy because of its object, Christ, or because of its subject, the believer who has faith *and perseveres in obedience*? In chapter 4, Simon Gathercole of the University of Cambridge and expert in early Christian studies offers us a concise survey of options in preparation for David VanDrunen's more dogmatic treatment of justifying faith in chapter 5. These chapters work together as VanDrunen, professor of systematic theology and Christian ethics at Westminster Seminary California, harnesses solid exegesis for a Reformational account of the "instrument" of justification.

Within American evangelicalism, however, there is a great deal of confusion even among Calvinists over this definition of justifying faith, some of which arises from a surprising source: the writings of the New England revivalist Jonathan Edwards. There have been numerous attempts to parse Edwards' understanding of faith found in his famous *Treatise on Justification*, and doubtlessly there will be many more due to his enduring popularity. But Princeton Theological Seminary Professor George Hunsinger offers the best straightforward analysis of Edwards available. In chapter 6 Hunsinger cuts to the chase and explains how Edwards is less reliable at points than traditional Reformed interpretations. This is not offered to alienate those who would call Edwards their "homeboy," as some t-shirts boast, but for the sake of redirecting some restless Calvinists away from an ambiguous text to the clarity of the earlier Reformed tradition, such as Calvin himself, the later Genevan theologian Francis Turretin, or even the writings of the biblical theologian Herman Witsius.[7] This reading of Edwards will be controversial, yet it is important to recognize where Reformation traditions begin and end in order to advance the discussion.

SHALL WE STILL PROTEST? THE DEBATE WITH ROME

In the next section, we explore how these topics have been taken up in the revival of ecumenical discussions between evangelicals and Roman Catholics. There is perhaps no better way to see the similarities and differences between mono-covenantalist doctrines of justification and the official Roman view as defined by the Council of Trent than by a fact-finding interview with Catholic apologist Robert Sungenis (chapter 7). Sungenis converted from Catholicism to Protestantism in his youth, studied at a Reformed seminary under Norman Shepherd, and has since returned to Rome. Chapter 8 features a critique of "Evangelicals and Catholics Together" initiatives by R. C. Sproul of Ligonier Ministries. This classic article restates the doctrine of imputation and points out the studied ambiguity on imputation that is at the heart of these various joint Protestant and Catholic declarations on salvation. Chapter 9 comprises a list of ten propositions on faith and salvation that reinforce Sproul's concerns for theological precision on faith, imputation, justification, and sanctification, all to help you know what you believe and why you believe it. In chapter 10, Lutheran statesman J. A. O. Preus III reminds us that the doctrine of justification is the article on which the Christian church either stands or falls.

UNION AND PEACE WITH GOD

Corresponding to the lumping and flattening of redemptive history by mono-covenantalists, there has been an attempt to replace the classical Protestant *order of salvation* with a single doctrine of believers' union with Christ. While the latter is certainly a crucial biblical doctrine, Westminster Seminary California Professor John V. Fesko argues in chapter 11 that union with Christ should not be used to blur important distinctions between Christ's active and passive obedience, and justification and sanctification. Here Fesko engages Wright and representatives of the Federal Vision, another movement that parallels without directly drawing from the New Perspective on Paul. There are other important distinctions to bear in mind as well, such as the crucial distinction between justification and sanctification. In chapter 12 Ken Jones, pastor of Glendale Missionary Baptist Church, demonstrates why such distinctions are not about scholastic gamemanship, but about protecting the heart of the gospel.

We then turn in chapter 13 to Calvin scholar Dennis Tamburello, a Roman Catholic and professor at Sienna College who offers an outsider's perspective on the legacy of the Reformed tradition for Christian theology. There is no special pleading here, and this reflection sets up a transition from the doctrine of justification to three concluding chapters on the promises and realities of the justified life, a life of peace with God in the pursuit of God, by Jerry Bridges from The Navigators (chapter 14), W. Robert Godfrey from Westminster Seminary California (chapter 15), and Harold J. Senkbeil from Concordia Theological Seminary (chapter 16). Personal holiness has always been a priority for Refor-mation Protestants, because God in his grace always produces fruit in the life of the justified sinner. Sometimes this is a forgotten or controverted point, and it certainly needs clarification—in our age and every age. Therefore, in chapter 17, Michael Horton takes up the present-day "holiness wars." In his conclusion, Horton leaves us with challenging answers to the ultimate and provocative question: Does justification still matter?

Modern Reformation has discussed these and many other important themes in every issue of our magazine going back twenty years. Readers who are familiar with us will not be surprised to read that we *continue* to believe that Reformation theology, rather than a hindrance, could actually be a great biblical resource for the present reform of our churches. If you are learning about us for the first time, we eagerly invite you to rally with us around the *"solas"* of the Reformation for the good of contemporary evangelicalism.

COVENANT

AND

JUSTIFICATION

CHAPTER 01

Covenant and Justification: Engaging N. T. Wright and John Piper

BY MICHAEL S. HORTON

P erhaps the most respected evangelical Jesus scholar, Bishop N. T. Wright has been stirring things up in Paul studies for nearly three decades. Although profiting from many of his insights, I have interacted critically with his treatment of justification in *Covenant and Salvation* (Westminster John Knox, 2007). My focus here, however, is on the importance of covenant theology as the context for justification, joining the conversation between John Piper and N. T. Wright.

In The Future of Justification: A Response to N. T. Wright (Crossway, 2007), Piper seems to regard Wright's treatment of the covenant motif in Paul as a distraction from the apostle's doctrine of justification. In his rejoinder, *Justification: God's Plan and Paul's Vision*, Wright counters that Paul's doctrine of justification is

> about what we may call the *covenant*—the covenant God made with Abraham, the covenant whose purpose was from the beginning the saving call of a worldwide family through whom God's saving purposes for the world were to be realized....For Piper, and many like him, the very idea of a covenant of this kind remains strangely foreign and alien....Despite the strong covenantal theology of John Calvin himself, and his positive reading of the story of Israel as fulfilled in Jesus Christ, many who claim Calvinist or Reformed heritage today resist applying it in the way that, as I argue in this book, Paul himself does, in line with the solid biblical foundations for the 'continuing exile' theme.[1]

While in my view the lion's share of false choices are on Wright's side of the ledger, I agree with his point that covenant theology is the proper context for Paul's doctrine of justification. My concern with Wright's view is not that he gives too much place for the covenantal motif—particularly, the unfolding of the Abrahamic covenant issuing in a cosmic redemption. In fact, I even find Wright's end-of-exile motif persuasive and enriching. Rather, my concern is that he reduces the complexity of this covenant theology, conflating law and gospel in a single covenant type—viz., *covenantal nomism*.[2]

Simply to advocate covenant theology does not necessarily specify its content. In 1991 Wright wrote that "covenant theology is one of the main clues, usually neglected, for understanding Paul."[3] Yet, at the same time, he is quick to distance his covenant theology from sixteenth- and seventeenth-century versions.[4] In a later work Wright concedes that he has never read these sources: "Like many New Testament scholars, I am largely ignorant of the Pauline exegesis of all but a few of the fathers and reformers. The Middle Ages, and the seventeenth and eighteenth centuries, had plenty to say about Paul, but I have not read it."[5] Classic covenant theology has therefore been, in my view, too lightly dismissed—even caricatured—without serious firsthand evaluation. While I agree with Wright's claim that covenant theology is more crucial for understanding justification than Piper suggests, I argue that it is Wright's version of covenant theology (viz., reducing different types to "covenantal nomism") that generates false choices.

SUMMARY OF CLASSIC COVENANT THEOLOGY

At least as defined by its confessions and dogmatic consensus, Reformed theology is synonymous with covenant theology. Only by ignoring the dominant architecture of Reformed theology can Wright contend that all forms of Reformation theology merely tack on the idea of covenant. Classic covenant (Reformed) theology begins with a *covenant of redemption* (*pactum salutis*) within the Trinity from eternity. In this pact between the persons of the Godhead, the Father gives to his Son an elect people with Christ as the Mediator and the Spirit as the person who unites the elect to the Son. All of the historical covenants serve this eternal purpose.

This federal theology gathers various biblical covenants under two broad types: law and promise, or the covenant of works and the covenant of grace. Sometimes referred to also as the covenant of law, nature, or creation, the original relationship of human beings to God was one of condescension, goodness, and kindness. Yet it was not a *gracious* covenant, because grace (like mercy) is God's attitude toward transgressors. Created in a state of justice, Adam was given a task to fulfill, with the Tree of Life as the reward for obedience. As the representative head, Adam would lead the whole creation in his train into the everlasting Sabbath rest—in other words, the consummation. Already we see the wide scope of covenantal interpretation: It is not only about individual salvation, reduced to "going to heaven when we die," but to the consummation of God's kingdom in cosmic-historical terms.

With Adam's transgression, humanity fell under the curse of this covenant, yet God graciously delayed the consummation (symbolized by the Tree of Life, now guarded by cherubim against reentry), opening up space for his redemptive plan centering around the promised deliverer—the Last Adam. This promise launched the *covenant of grace*. Though exiled from Eden, Adam and Eve were given faith in God's promise, and Seth and his covenantal line are distinguished by the fact that "at that time people began to call on the name of the Lord" (Gen. 4:26).

In fulfillment of his promise to Abraham, Yahweh has acted in and through his people Israel to redeem a worldwide family of sinners. Like the *protoeuangelion* of Genesis 3:15–16, the covenant that Yahweh swore to Abraham was unilateral and utterly gracious in its basis. However, the covenant that the people swore at Mount Sinai was qualitatively distinct from the covenant that Yahweh swore to Abraham. Although everlasting rest in the true Canaan was attained by grace alone through faith alone (according to the Abrahamic covenant), the nation of Israel was under a covenant of law: "Do this and you shall live." Like Adam, Israel was God's servant, entrusted with the commission to cleanse God's garden of sin and to expand his righteous reign to the ends of the earth; but "like Adam, Israel sinned and broke my covenant" (Hos. 6:7).

Yet God made a promise through the prophets on the basis of another covenant (in continuity with the promise made to Abraham). In Jeremiah 31, it is expressly said that this "new covenant...will not be like the covenant that I made with the children of Israel in the wilderness, which they broke" (v. 31). God himself will transfer the guilt of his people to the Suffering Servant, and he will transfer to them the righteousness of this obedient Son (Isa. 53). In the new covenant, Yahweh himself will be the Mediator and will act in judgment and justification, bringing salvation to the earth (Isa. 59; Jer. 23:5–6; 33:16; with 1 Cor. 2:30–31; 2 Cor. 5:21). Therefore, not by setting aside the covenant of works but by fulfilling all righteousness and bearing the sanctions on our behalf, the Last Adam wins the right for himself and for his posterity to eat from the Tree of Life.

"God justifies the wicked" (Rom. 4:5). Israel is in precisely the same condition as the rest of humanity, lying under the curse of the law. The law reveals the righteousness that God is in his very nature, but the gospel announces the gift of righteousness that God gives in his Son through faith (Rom. 3:24–25; Gal. 2:21; Phil. 3:8–9; and so forth). "Therefore, since we have been justified by faith, we have peace with God through our Lord Jesus Christ" (Rom. 5:1).

From the period of development to the present, Reformed theologians have debated the finer points (particularly the relation of the Sinai covenant to the covenant of grace). Nevertheless, a consensus emerged (evident, for example, in the Westminster Confession) affirming the three covenants I have mentioned: the eternal covenant of redemption; the covenant of works; and the covenant of grace. With these last two covenants, Reformed theology affirmed (with Lutheranism) the crucial distinction between law and gospel, but within a more concrete biblical-historical framework.[6]

A TALE OF TWO COVENANTS: A SUMMARY OF ANCIENT NEAR EASTERN RESEARCH ON "COVENANT"

Ironically, just at the moment when so much Protestant biblical scholarship is rejecting a sharp distinction between law and gospel, Ancient Near Eastern scholars from Jewish and Roman Catholic traditions have demonstrated the accuracy of that seminal distinction between covenants of law and covenants of promise.[7]

As Moshe Weinfeld pointed out in his important 1970 essay, Israel's history is determined by a covenantal tradition in the form of *royal grant* on the one hand and the *suzerainty treaty* on the other, both well attested in Ancient Near Eastern diplomacy.[8]

Having rescued a lesser ruler ("vassal") from the jaws of an oppressor, the suzerain (or "great king") would annex the tribe or kingdom to his empire, imposing a new constitution. Hence, it is called a suzerainty treaty. It is imposed unilaterally by the sovereign; the vassal is in no position to bargain, and he accepts all the obligations as well as the curses for violating the treaty. Included in such ancient Hittite formularies were the following features: 1) preamble (identifying the suzerain who made the treaty); 2) a historical prologue (justifying the suzerain's claims over the vassal's realm); 3) stipulations (commands); and 4) sanctions (curses for violation, blessings for obedience). Such treaties typically involved public ceremonies in which the new relationship was ratified and the treaty-tablets were deposited in the religious shrines of both parties, over which their respective deities witnessed in judgment.

The royal grant was a gift bestowed by the suzerain upon a vassal, usually in view of past performance on the suzerain's behalf—not unlike the peerages bestowed by monarchs in more recent times. Royal grants were "an outright gift by a king to a subject."[9]

Covenant of Law

Ancient Near Eastern scholars have recognized the close similarities between the Sinai covenant and suzerainty treaties, in both form and content. On the basis of military intervention, the vassal is obligated to obey all the stipulations imposed by the new suzerain.[10] Even the solemn ratification ceremonies are similar, as they are transferred from the political realm of international treaties to the covenant between Yahweh and his people. As G. E. Mendenhall notes, "One ceremony is the sprinkling of blood upon altar and people, another is the banquet in the presence of Yahweh." Furthermore, "The tradition of the deposit of the law in the Ark of the Covenant is certainly connected with the covenant customs of pre-Mosaic times."[11] Given the equation of gossip or untrusting speech or conduct with breach of the covenant stipulations in the Hittite treaty, "The traditions of the 'murmurings' in the wilderness is also a motif which receives new meaning in the light of the covenant."[12] In fact, the exact form is followed in Exodus 20 as well as in Deuteronomy 5: Yahweh identifies himself as the suzerain (preamble), with a brief historical prologue citing his deliverance of the people from Egypt, followed by the Ten Commandments (stipulations), with clear warnings (sanctions) about violating the treaty to which they have sworn their allegiance. The covenant of Joshua 24 follows this pattern as well.

After the Fall, of course, all of God's acts of kindness were gracious and merciful. This is especially true of God's election and deliverance of Israel. In fulfillment of his promise to Abraham, God delivered his people from Egypt and in spite of their sin brought them into the typological land of promise. Before entering, they were warned not to imagine they had been given this land as a reward for their own righteousness (Deut. 7:6–8). Nevertheless, at Sinai they swore allegiance to all of the stipulations of God's law, not merely as a response of gratitude but as a condition for their blessing in the land. Yahweh himself will drive the nation of Israel out of his land if they fail to keep the terms of the treaty (vv. 9–11). Therefore, E. P. Sanders's well-known formula "Get in by grace, stay in by obedience," and the term he coins for this type of arrangement *covenantal nomism*, appear entirely justified by the form and content of this suzerainty treaty.[13] Yahweh's relationship with Israel was marital: simultaneously legal and deeply personal, yet divorce was always a real possibility in the case of adulterous breach.

At Sinai, Moses recited the words of the law he had received, and the people "answered with one voice, and said, 'All the words that the Lord has spoken we will do.'" Writing down the words, he set up an altar (the vassal's archive) with twelve pillars corresponding to the twelve tribes. After the people took the oath, "All this we will do and we will be obedient," Moses sprinkled the blood on the people "and said, 'See the blood of the covenant that the Lord has made with you in accordance with all these words'" (Exod. 24:3–8).

The character of this covenant could not be more vividly portrayed: Israel had made the oath and it was sealed by Moses' act of splashing the blood on the people, with the ominous warning that this act implied.[14]

The Sinai covenant itself, then, is a law-covenant. The land is *given* to Israel, but for the purpose of *fulfilling* its covenantal vocation. Remaining in the land is therefore conditional on Israel's personal performance of the stipulations the people swore at Sinai. Though beyond the scope of this chapter, the parallels between Adam's commission and Israel's become especially striking in the lawsuit brought by the prophets.

The ultimate promise of a worldwide family of Abraham—sinners justified and glorified in a renewed creation—is unconditional in its basis, while the continuing existence of the national theocracy as a type of that everlasting covenant depended on Israel's obedience. The ceremonies of the law pointed to Christ and his gospel, but the terms of remaining in the typological land as that beacon to the world was conditional on obedience. Yahweh imposed the conditions with the promise of life for obedience and death for disobedience, but did not accept any conditions.

The conditional language is evident throughout the Torah: If you do this, you will live; if you fail to do this, you will die (Lev. 18:5; Deut. 4:1; 5:33; 6:24–25; 8:1; 30:15–18; Neh. 9:29; Ezra 18:19; 20:11–21; and so forth). The form and content are those of a suzerainty covenant and are evident also in the covenant between God and Adam (Gen. 2:16–17). Like Adam, Israel had a mission to undertake, a task to perform, a destiny to realize not only for itself but for the whole world, and this vocation was Israel's either to keep or to lose.

Covenant of Promise

The Decalogue and Joshua 24 fit this suzerainty pattern, but as Mendenhall observes, "it can readily be seen that the covenant with Abraham (and Noah) is of completely different form." In Genesis 15 and 17, *God* is the oath-maker and his covenant is ratified by the vision of God—the suzerain—passing through the pieces in self-malediction. Abram believes and is justified (Gen. 15:6). Mendenhall notes that even circumcision is "a sign of the covenant, like the rainbow in Genesis 9," identifying the recipient of such a gift. Yahweh gives Abram ("father") a new name (Abraham, "father of many"), and this becomes paradigmatic for the covenant of promise to the end of the age (Gen. 35:10; Isa. 45:4; 62:6; Rev. 2:17). "The covenant of Moses, on the other hand, is almost the exact opposite," Mendenhall adds. "It imposes specific obligations upon the tribes or clans without binding Yahweh to specific obligations, though it goes without saying that the covenant relationship itself presupposed the protection and support of Yahweh to Israel."[15] The ceremony of splashing blood on the Israelites in accordance with their oath, "All this we will do," fits a suzerainty treaty perfectly. However, the theophany in which God passes through the pieces in Genesis 15 is unprecedented in these international treaties.[16]

On the basis of the Sinai covenant, the prophets prosecute God's lawsuit against Israel and Judah. On that basis, there is no hope. In fact, God says, "And those who transgressed my covenant and did not keep the terms of the covenant that *they made* before me, I will make like the calf when they cut it in two and passed between its parts; the officials of Judah, the officials of Jerusalem, the eunuchs, the priests, and all the people of the land who passed between the parts of the calf shall be handed over to their enemies and to those who seek their lives" (Jer. 34:18–20, emphasis added). Hope is indeed held out beyond the exile, but it is always on the basis of God's unilateral promise of grace ("for the sake of the promise I made to Abraham" or "to David"), not the conditional covenant that Israel swore at Sinai.

Although it pledged common grace rather than redemption from sin, the Noahic covenant too was a one-sided promise on God's part with no conditions attached (Gen. 9). This pattern can be seen also in God's promise to David and to his heirs. In the period of the monarchy, Yahweh was the *witness* in the anointing of the king.[17] Now, however, "the tradition of the covenant with Abraham became the pattern of a covenant between Yahweh and David, whereby *Yahweh promised* to maintain the Davidic line on the throne (II Sam. 23:5)." No matter what David and his descendants did or failed to do vis-à-vis the Sinaitic covenant, God will unilaterally and unconditionally preserve an heir on his throne. "Yahweh bound Himself, exactly as in the Abrahamic and Noachite covenant, and therefore Israel could not escape responsibility to the king. The covenant with Abraham was the 'prophecy' and that with David the 'fulfillment.'"[18] This too is a royal grant, an inheritance that the suzerain gives to the undeserving vassal and to his heirs.

Steven L. McKenzie sheds further light on the obvious differences between the Sinaitic and Davidic covenants in terms of their conditional versus promissory character. In 2 Samuel 7, the pure divine condescension (promissory covenant) is underscored (especially v. 5, with the emphatic "you"). David wants to build a house for God, but the Davidic covenant is a unilateral promise from God to build a house for David. The narrative makes Yahweh appear stern and unwilling to receive his servant's well-meant zeal, but the rationale is clear. God knows what David is like, and he knows what his heirs will be like as well. The Abrahamic covenant will not be realized in history if it is in any way dependent on the zeal of his sinful people. If the promise is going to become a reality, it is Yahweh himself who will have to make it happen. "It is this promise of an eternal royal line that essentially constitutes the covenant with David," McKenzie notes.[19] As soon as David's own son arrives on the scene, the vassal is unworthy and yet the treaty is unaffected (1 Kings 11:33). Israel had, for all intents and purposes, so violated the treaty that Yahweh's continued presence could only be explained as "for the sake of my servant David" (2 Kings 8:19; 18:34; 20:6)—which, penultimately, means the same as "for the sake of the fathers/Abraham," and ultimately in retrospect (i.e., looking back from the New Testament) "for the sake of Christ"—the promised seed of Abraham and David (Gal. 3:16; Rom. 1:3). This highlights the significance of the genealogy in Matthew 1:1–17 and the angelic announcement to Mary in Luke 1:32 that "God will give him the throne of his father David."

Only with the eighth-century prophets did the Sinai covenant return to the foreground, along with the correspondences to the Hittite treaties. It was "back to the federation," and the rediscovery of the "Book of the Law" led to "a thorough house-cleaning."

> The king [Josiah] together with the people entered into covenant (before the Lord: i.e., with Yahweh as witness, not as a party to the covenant) to keep the commandments of the Lord....It brought home to Josiah and the religious leadership that they had been living in a fool's paradise in their assumption that Yahweh had irrevocably committed Himself to preserve the nation in the Davidic-Abrahamic covenant. Moses was rediscovered after having been dormant for nearly three and a half centuries.[20]

They were astonished to realize that the covenant "provided for curses as well as blessings (II Kings 22:13)."[21] In other words, the returning exiles were surprised to learn that the national covenant was conditional on their obedience rather than being an unconditional grant.

The point is this: *The deepest distinction in Scripture is not between the Old and New Testaments but between the covenants of law and the covenants of promise that run throughout both.* The two covenant traditions are distinguished in form and content, even throughout the same unfolding history of redemption.

Mendenhall writes, "The harmonization of the two covenant traditions meant that great emphasis had to be placed upon the divine forgiveness, and this becomes the foundation of the New Covenant predicted by Jeremiah." He adds, "The New Covenant of Christianity obviously continued the tradition of the Abrahamic-

Davidic covenant with its emphasis upon the Messiah, Son of David. Paul uses the covenant of Abraham to show the temporary validity of the Mosaic covenant."[22]

Moses is the mediator of the Sinai covenant, but even he is listed among the heirs of promise along with Abraham through faith in Christ (Heb. 11:23–28). It is striking that this passage in Hebrews does not include any reference to the Sinai covenant. Rather, Moses "considered abuse suffered for the Christ to be greater wealth than the treasures of Egypt, for he was looking ahead to the reward. By faith he left Egypt….By faith he kept the Passover and the sprinkling of blood, so that the destroyer of the firstborn would not touch the firstborn of Egypt" (vv. 26–28). As Abraham by faith looked beyond the promise of an earthly land to a heavenly one, Moses apprehended Christ by faith even through the shadows of the law.

Relating Sinai (Law) and Zion (Gospel)

Therefore, the distinction between law and gospel or between the covenant of works and the covenant of grace is not the result of imposing an alien sixteenth-century construct on the biblical text. In fact, it is the reduction of these distinct covenants to a single type that gives rise to a central dogma (covenantal nomism). Even some scholars who share Wright's commitment to covenantal nomism at least recognize the distinction between covenants of law and promise, correlated with suzerainty treaties and royal grants, respectively. I will refer briefly to two of these examples: the eminent Jewish scholar Jon D. Levenson and Pope Benedict XVI.

JON D. LEVENSON

According to Levenson, the Sinai covenant was a "bilateral relationship," conditional on obedience, with Moses as their mediator.[23] The promise is given in Exodus 19:6: "You shall be to me a kingdom of priests and a holy nation," which is "a reward for loyalty in covenant" dependent on Israel's oath, "All that Yahweh has spoken we will do!"[24] "Awareness of divine grace sets the stage for the stipulations," but Israel must fulfill the law's conditions to remain in the land of blessing.[25] The covenant in Joshua 24 repeats the Sinai conditions. "YHWH has brought Israel success up to now, but if she abandons him and serves another suzerain, he will in turn reverse himself and annihilate Israel."[26]

Levenson treats as a settled scholarly consensus the view that Israel's national covenant was a suzerainty treaty.[27] He also recognizes the different key sounded in the prophets when they speak of a "new covenant." In Hosea 2, for example, Levenson points out that Yahweh makes a new covenant not just with Israel but with all living things and that "God assumes the Mosaic office of covenant mediator," guaranteeing its security. "But we hear nothing of the curses, for the vision is one of redemption through covenant, and the assumption seems to be that, where God mediates and thus guarantees covenant, the stipulations will be fulfilled as a matter of course."[28] By the way, the emphasis that Levenson places on *Yahweh's* personal mediation as that which distinguishes the new covenant from the old bears striking similarity with the argument in Hebrews: this eternal covenant is conditional only on Yahweh's faithfulness and secured by his sole mediation.[29]

On the one hand, Levenson affirms a clear distinction between the Sinaitic and Davidic covenants. The latter establishes an everlasting dynasty of Davidic heirs. As "a pledge of divine support for a human dynasty," which is "something almost unthinkable in the case of Sinai," the Davidic covenant belongs to Zion, rather than to Sinai, Levenson observes.[30] He even acknowledges, with other scholars I have cited, that "the Davidic covenant does not follow, even loosely, the formulary characteristic of the suzerainty treaty upon which so many of the texts dealing with the Sinaitic covenant are modeled....Their moral record is in no way essential to the validity of the covenant."[31] And Levenson goes on, appealing to Weinfeld, to elaborate the differences between the suzerainty treaty and the "covenant of grant," noting the parallel, both in form and content, between the Davidic covenant and the unilateral covenants that God made with Noah and Abraham. He concludes, "This Davidic covenant, then, is distinct in kind from the Sinaitic."[32]

Each covenant is so profoundly distinct, it practically generates different ontological frames of reference. While the Sinai covenant is fragile, a covenant of law dependent on Israel's obedience, the covenants with Abraham and David are secured in heaven forever on the basis of God's royal grant. "And since the focus is upon the constancy of God rather than the changeability of man, it brings to light what is secure and inviolable, whereas the Sinaitic texts tend to emphasize the precariousness of life and the consequent need for a continuously reinvigorated obedience."[33] Hence "for the sake of David," even bad kings rule (1 Kings 15:4; 2 Kings 8:19). The everlasting promise trumps the moral conduct of its heirs. "Jerusalem and...especially Mount Zion, are a sign that beneath and beyond the pain and chaos of the realm we call history, there is another realm, upheld by the indefectible promise of God. Dynasty and Temple, the house of David and house of God, function within the order of history, but are rooted in that other order of things."[34] In the prophets (see Isa. 29:1–8; Jer. 7:1–15), the earthly Zion is violable, the heavenly one inviolable.[35] "The Temple exists and functions in the spiritual universe by his grace alone."[36]

With this background from Levenson, Paul's contrast in Galatians 4 between "two covenants" (law and promise) in terms of two mountains (earthly Jerusalem, now corresponding to Sinai; heavenly Jerusalem, corresponding to Zion) and two mothers (Hagar and Sarah, respectively) is all the more significant. So, too, is the contrast drawn in the book of Hebrews between the "old covenant" and the "better covenant" whose mediator is God himself, heavenly, and inviolable: Zion rather than Sinai (see especially 12:18–29).

Levenson acknowledges that there is no way of getting around the fact that "the Sinaitic and Davidic covenants, at least as the latter appears in 2 Samuel 7 and Psalm 89, are of radically different types. The former is a *treaty*; the latter is a *grant*. Since covenant was not a unitary concept in ancient Israel, the use of the term should not be taken to indicate an integrative movement." In contrast to Sinai, the Davidic covenant "is an alliance between YHWH and David, not with Israel per se." [37] (The close relationship between Abraham and David, as representing promise-covenants, is also affirmed by Paul's point in Galatians 3:16 that God made the promise to Abraham's *seed*, meaning Christ, not to *seeds*, meaning individual Israelites.)

However, in each of these instances where his careful exegesis leads to a clear distinction between covenants and even the triumph of Zion over Sinai, Levenson asserts the ultimacy of Sinai over Zion and therefore of law over promise. The Abrahamic, Davidic, and new covenants all become absorbed into the Sinaitic covenant.[38] Even though his own exegesis of Hosea 2 suggests otherwise, his basic commitment to covenantal nomism leads him to conclude that this new covenant is simply "the gracious offer to Israel to reenter the legal/erotic relationship and the renewed willingness of Israel to do so."[39] The goal of the various covenant renewals after the exile, says Levenson, "is to induce Israel to step into the position of the generation of Sinai, in other words, to actualize the past so that this new generation will become the Israel of the classic covenant relationship (cf. Deut. 30:19–20)."[40] In fact, Levenson's thesis can be summarized in his statement, "There is, therefore, no voice more central to Judaism than the voice heard on Mount Sinai."[41] It is the suzerainty covenant that has the last word. "The covenant without stipulations, the Abrahamic covenant of Genesis 15 and 17, is only a preparation for the Sinaitic covenant, into which it is absorbed."[42] With great insight, though at variance with the New Perspective on Paul, Levenson notes, "If the Davidic covenant never displaced the Sinaitic in the Hebrew Bible, it did, in a sense, in the New Testament."[43]

If Levenson accurately represents the views of early Judaism, then this interpretation (especially the last sentence) underscores the accuracy of the New Testament charge we find especially in Paul: namely, that Judaism—and the "Judaizing" party within the church—had assimilated the Abrahamic covenant of promise to the Sinai law-covenant (see especially Gal. 3:15–18). Gospel had been absorbed into law. Although he has recognized as contrasting categories the "Mosaic/Sinaitic and the Davidic/Zionistic orientations," he says that the priority of the former over the latter is precisely where Judaism and Christianity part ways. "In fact, the Davidic theology is the origin of Jewish messianism and the christology of the church."[44] The Sinai legacy, according to Levenson, rather than being the "schoolmaster" to lead us to Christ, is integrated into the Zion tradition in that the Messiah will come with "Israel's observance of the stipulations of Sinai."[45]

If one confuses the principle by which the national promises of land, temple, and kingdom are upheld (the people's obedience) with the principle by which the heavenly reality to which these types pointed was inherited (sheer promise by virtue of the obedience of the covenant head), then salvation (whether corporate or individual) comes through "the works of the law" (Sinai) rather than through "the faith of Abraham." Such distinctions between gift and contract are clearly in Paul's mind, for example, in Romans 4:4–5.

This is a good place to remind ourselves that in the covenant theology of the Reformed tradition, these two covenants and "mountains" meet in Christ, who as the covenantal *head* fulfills the Sinaitic law (already anticipated in the Adamic covenant) and as the covenant *mediator* dispenses the fruit of his labors to his heirs in a covenant of grace.[46] Rather than set aside the law-covenant, he fulfills it (positively) and bears its curses (negatively), so the inheritance can legitimately (legally) be conferred on the terms of grace alone (the royal grant).

POPE BENEDICT XVI

Pope Benedict XVI also acknowledges a distinction between law-covenants and promise-covenants in the same terms, drawing on many of the same sources I have cited. He rightly emphasizes the unity of the two testaments: law and gospel do not correspond to Old and New Testaments in any sort of Marcionite opposition.[47] He even notes that there is no single definition of *berith* [covenant]; the meaning "can only be gathered from the particular biblical contexts."[48] Although the Sinai covenant was an "act of God's love,"[49] the New Testament "sees the covenant made with Abraham as the real, fundamental, and abiding covenant; according to Paul, the covenant made with Moses was interposed (Rom. 5:20) 430 years after the Abrahamic covenant (Gal. 3:17); it could not abrogate the covenant with Abraham but constituted only an intermediary stage in God's providential plan."[50]

On the one hand, Benedict's exegesis leads him to conclude that "Paul distinguishes very sharply between two kinds of covenant that we find in the Old Testament": "a covenant that consists of legal prescriptions and the covenant that is essentially a promise, the gift of friendship, bestowed without conditions." In fact, "*Whereas the covenant imposing obligations is patterned on the vassal contract, the covenant of promise has the royal grant as its model.* To that extent Paul, with his contrast between the covenant with Abraham and the covenant with Moses, has rightly interpreted the biblical text" (emphasis added).[51] "The conditional covenant, which depended on man's faithful observance of the Law, is replaced by the unconditional covenant in which God binds himself irrevocably. We are unmistakably here in the same conceptual milieu as we found earlier in 2 Corinthians, with its contrast between two covenants."[52] Benedict even appears to contradict his earlier statement that the new covenant inaugurated in the Upper Room is a renewal of the Sinaitic covenant when he adds,

> The Old Covenant is conditional: since it depends on the keeping of the Law, that is, on man's behavior; it can be broken and has been broken. Since its essential content is the Law, it is expressed in the formulation, "If you do all this...." This "if" draws man's changeable will into the very essence of the covenant itself and thus makes it a provisional covenant. By contrast, the covenant sealed in the Last Supper, in its inner essence, seems 'new' in the sense of the prophetic promise: it is not a contract with conditions but the gift of friendship, irrevocably bestowed. Instead of law we have grace.[53]

Remarkably, Benedict even acknowledges the proximity of this interpretation to the Reformation perspective:

> The rediscovery of Pauline theology at the Reformation laid special emphasis on this point: not works, but faith; not man's achievement, but the free bestowal of God's goodness. It emphatically underlined, therefore, that what was involved was not a "covenant" but a "testament," a pure decision and act on God's part. This is the context in which we must understand the teaching that it is God alone who does everything. (All the *solus* terms—*solus Deus*, *solus Christus*—must be understood in this context.)[54]

Therefore,

> With regard to the Sinai covenant, we must again draw a distinction....It is strictly limited to the people of Israel; it gives this nation a legal and cultic order (the two are inseparable) that as such cannot simply be extended to all nations. Since the juridical order is constitutive of the Sinai covenant, the law's "if" is part of its essence. To that extent, it is conditional, that is, temporal; within God's providential rule it is a stage that has its own allocated period of time. Paul set this forth very clearly, and no Christian can revoke it; history itself confirms this view.[55]

Thus, like Levenson, Benedict recognizes a sharp distinction between promise and law at the level of exegesis, even correlating it with the Abrahamic and Sinai covenants, respectively.

On the other hand, also like Levenson, Benedict finally surrenders these exegetical insights to the dogma of covenantal nomism, assimilating the gospel to law. "The covenant with Moses is incorporated into the covenant with Abraham, and the Law becomes a mediator of promise....The one Covenant is realized in the plurality of covenants."[56] Law simply becomes a form of gospel—in fact, "the Law itself is the concrete form of grace. For to know God's will is grace."[57] The new covenant that is ratified at the Last Supper "is *the prolongation of the Sinai covenant, which is not abrogated, but renewed*" (emphasis added).[58]

In addition to contradicting his earlier exegesis, however, Benedict's interpretation subverts the point of Jeremiah 31:32 that the new covenant "will *not* be like" the Sinai treaty that Israel broke. It also fails to appreciate the asymmetry between the "blood of the covenant" splashed on the Israelites at Sinai in confirmation of their oath ("All this we will do") and Jesus' inauguration of the new covenant in *his* blood (as if to say, "All this I will do"). Finally, it fails to appreciate the significance of the New Testament claim that the Sinai covenant, having been fulfilled, is now "obsolete" (Heb. 8:12–13).

DISTINGUISHING THE COVENANTS

I have chosen these two conversation partners to make the point that the distinction between the covenant of works and the covenant of grace is probably more generally supported by scholars today than in any previous period. Even when a dogmatic commitment to covenantal nomism overrides it, sound exegesis demands it. The irony, however, is that many Protestant exegetes today simply adopt covenantal nomism without even wrestling with the distinctions in the way we have seen with Levenson and Pope Benedict. Walter Brueggemann, for example, rejects the attempt to distinguish conditional and unconditional aspects as an intrusion of the Pelagian debate. Rather, he says we should treat "covenant" as a univocal concept. "Thus I suggest that E. P. Sanders's term *covenantal nomism* is about right, because it subsumes law (*nomos*) under the rubric of covenant. By inference, I suggest that grace must also be subsumed under covenant."[59] This question lies at the heart of the debates over justification. Is the promissory covenant subsumed under (or absorbed into) the covenant of law, resulting in a covenantal nomism? Or are these two covenants always distinguished and, on the point of justification, to be treated in fact as antithetical means of inheriting eternal life?

It is not Paul who introduces a law-promise, Sinai-Abraham, Moses-Christ contrast. Following the prophets, Jesus enacts in his teaching and actions the redefinition of the people of God around himself rather than Moses. By justifying the wicked by faith apart from works of the law, God will finally be able to realize the promise made to Abraham and heralded by the prophets (Isa. 9; 49; 60; 66; Jer. 4:2; Ezek. 39) that in him and his Seed all the nations of the earth will be blessed.

In classic covenant theology, then, the questions of Gentile inclusion in the people of God, the removal of boundary markers, and the fulfillment of the promise of Abraham's worldwide family are addressed. However, they are the consequence of justification. In Wright's approach, the ecclesiological question is the main thing and justification is a consequence. Yet apart from the legal basis that justification (i.e., imputation) provides, the union of Jew and Gentile in Christ is suspended in midair. In spite of dogmatic commitment to covenantal nomism, Jewish and Roman Catholic scholars recognize that there is an obvious contrast between covenants of law and promise, not only in Paul but in the Hebrew scriptures. Restricting the "works of the law" to ethnic boundary markers and the new covenant's good news to the inclusion of Gentiles in Abraham's worldwide family simply does not make sense of the deeper contrast between law and promise as covenantal principles of inheritance. It not only fails to make sense of a passage such as 2 Corinthians 3, but also of Jeremiah 31, which it glosses.

After comparing the Abrahamic promise to a last will and testament in Galatians, Paul says,

> Now the promises were made to Abraham and to his seed; it does not say, "And to seeds," as of many; but it says, "And to your seed," that is, to one person, who is Christ. My point is this: the law, which came four hundred thirty years later, does not annul a covenant previously ratified by God, so as to nullify the promise. For if the inheritance comes from the law, it no longer comes from the promise; but God granted it to Abraham through the promise. (Gal. 3:15–18)

Thus for Paul, there are two ways of inheriting the divine estate: law and promise. Each excludes or nullifies the other when the question arises as to how one obtains the eternal inheritance of the heavenly Jerusalem. "Now this is an allegory: these women are two covenants," of "law" and "promise," respectively, standing for "the present Jerusalem...in slavery with her children," and "the Jerusalem above; she is free, and she is our mother" (Gal. 4:21–27).

Consequently, that which stands in the way of the unification of all of God's elect, Jew and Gentile, in one body—which is of such concern in Paul's mission—is not simply the ceremonial laws defining ethnic boundaries, but the law-covenant as such. It is not that the moral laws of the Decalogue are to be set aside, but that with respect to *the method for obtaining the inheritance* law is to be strictly opposed to the principle of faith in the promise that God has done everything already in Christ.

> Just as Abraham "believed God, and it was reckoned to him as righteousness," so, you see, those who believe are the descendants of Abraham. And the scripture, foreseeing that God would justify the Gentiles by faith, declared the gospel beforehand to Abraham, saying, "All the Gentiles shall be blessed in you." For this reason, those who believe are blessed with Abraham who believed. (Gal. 3:6–9)

The average Israelite under the old covenant stood in a gracious relationship with God, looking through the sacrifices in faith toward the Lamb of God, and also in a conditional relationship with God in terms of national status in the land.

The danger lies in conflating these two covenants, so that the temporary and conditional terms of the Sinai covenant become the basis for justification and the inheritance of the heavenly Jerusalem. At the Jerusalem Council, Peter did not seem to have assumed that the works of the law were restricted to ethnic boundary markers when he asked, "Now therefore why are you putting God to the test by placing on the neck of the disciples a yoke that neither our ancestors nor we have been able to bear? On the contrary, we believe that we will be saved through the grace of the Lord Jesus, just as they will" (Acts 15:7–11). No less than Paul is Peter's contrast between *the yoke of the law* and *salvation by grace in Christ alone*, not just ethnic boundaries and covenant membership.

It is converts among the Jewish Diaspora as well as Gentile believers who are addressed by Peter as those "who have been chosen and destined by God the Father and sanctified by the Spirit to be obedient to Jesus Christ and to be sprinkled with his blood" (1 Pet. 1:2). The allusion to Moses' liturgical act of sprinkling the people with the blood of the Sinai covenant is obvious, although in this case it is the greater blood of a greater mediator and a greater covenant. Believers are sprinkled with his blood not to ratify their words, "All this we will do," but in order to ratify his words to the Father that we find in his prayer: "I have accomplished everything that you gave me to do....And for their sakes I sanctify myself, so that they also may be sanctified in truth" (John 17:4, 19). These believers, Peter relates, are "living stones" being built into "a spiritual house," "a chosen race, a royal priesthood, a holy nation," even though they were "once not a people" and "had not received mercy" (1 Pet. 2:5; 9–10). Thus, it is in Christ and by his Spirit that the prophecy of a new covenant is fulfilled, a covenant that "will not be like the covenant that I made with their fathers" at Sinai (Jer. 31:32).

Only through this covenant of promise and royal grant is it possible for Israel, now (like the Gentiles) "dead in trespasses and sins," to be raised again to life as a new people, not only resuscitated but reborn as part of the new creation. Furthermore, it is only in such a "new and living way" that the promise of universal blessing given to Abraham can be realized through his Seed. And it was the confession of the earliest church that this is precisely what had occurred in the life, death, resurrection, and ascension of Christ—that it was, in fact, the firstfruits of this long-expected world to come.

Renewal of the entire cosmos is rooted in atoning sacrifice, justification, and adoption that reach their climax in the "revealing of the children of God" (Rom. 8:19). Even salvation from the exile of death itself is merely the consequence of a more basic liberation, precisely because death is not a natural threat but a covenantal sanction. "The sting of death is sin, and the power of sin is the law. But thanks be to God, who gives us the victory through our Lord Jesus Christ" (1 Cor. 15:56).

CONCLUSION: COVENANT THEOLOGY AND JUSTIFICATION

Asked to summarize his fundamental difference from Piper's approach to Paul, Wright responded, "Well, I set justification within the larger Pauline context, where it always comes, of God's purposes to fulfill his covenant promise to Abraham and so to rescue the whole creation, humankind of course centrally included, from sin and death. Piper holds that Abrahamic context at arm's length."[60]

In this concluding section, I will present three examples of how classic covenant theology, fortified by recent scholarship, can clarify rather than obscure Paul's teaching on justification.

Imputation

The first example is the issue of imputation. Wright often accuses others of reading Paul through the lens of tradition, giving the impression that he is merely "thinking Paul's thoughts after him." Piper points out that it is just as possible for biblical theology as it is for systematic theology to impose its own constructs on exegesis.[61] According to Piper, Wright's category of covenant functions in just this way, as a central dogma from which everything else—including justification—is deduced. Piper suggests, "For N. T. Wright, God's covenant with Israel is the dominant concept for understanding Paul and justification"; but as Piper points out, there is no reference to which covenant Wright has in mind.[62] As I see it, that is precisely the heart of the matter. The problem, then, is not with Wright's insistence on the importance of the covenantal motif—particularly the centrality of the Abrahamic covenant—but with his tendency to run these different covenants together in a way that excludes key aspects of Paul's arguments.

While I agree that Wright too often assumes Paul's continuity with Second Temple Judaism, Piper seems too wary of the role that Wright gives to the Abrahamic covenant.[63] Piper challenges Wright's view that "the covenant is the overarching category for understanding the great story of redemption, and [that] the law-court metaphor is a subordinate but integral part of it."[64] It is on this point, however, that I agree wholeheartedly with Wright. Law-court language has meaning in the Bible only within the covenantal context. But *which* covenantal context? The Abrahamic or the Sinaitic? It seems that for Wright, as for Jon Levenson and Pope Benedict, these covenants run together just as they did for many Jewish Christians in the early church. The problem is not *covenant theology* in general, but *covenantal nomism* in particular.

Wright's primary objection to the imputation of Christ's active obedience is that it's a category mistake: "If we use the language of the law-court, it makes no sense whatever to say that the judge imputes, imparts, bequeaths, conveys or otherwise transfers his righteousness to either the plaintiff or the defendant. Righteousness is not an object, a substance or gas which can be passed across the courtroom....To imagine the defendant somehow receiving the judge's righteousness is simply a category mistake."[65]

Piper replies first by arguing that God's glory is the motivating factor behind God's righteousness and all of his other attributes, much less the covenant.[66]

Yet, abstracted from the covenantal narrative, even God's glory can become a speculative "central dogma." Piper writes,

> God's righteousness, before there was a covenant, determined that punishment for sin would be part of what happens in the covenant (and outside it!). And notice also that the flow of the context from Romans 3:9*ff.* suggests that the "passing over of sins" in Romans 3:25 was not just the passing over of the sins of the covenant people Israel (see also Acts 14:15; 17:30), but of the nations as well. Therefore, limiting the "righteousness of God" in this context to covenantal categories is too narrow. [67]

Yet once again, it seems to me that the problem is not Wright's appeal to covenantal categories, but his reduction of the two covenant types to one. Of course, no one denies that God is eternally righteous. In classic covenant theology, however, God's righteousness could not have determined that punishment was required apart from a covenantal context that identified stipulations and sanctions. Humankind was created in a covenant of law. Although God's commands are consistent with his nature, sanctions (blessing and curse) are put into effect only in a covenant (see, for example, Rom. 7:7–10). By the way, this supports the classic federal argument for the covenant of works in creation, as well as Paul's broader argument in Romans that Israel is precisely in the same condition as the rest of humanity: "in Adam."

Wright says that "Paul's doctrine of justification is focused on the divine law-court," over against "the supposed moral achievement of Jesus in gaining, through his perfect obedience, a righteousness which can then be passed on to his faithful people."[68] So Wright interprets the law-court in a covenantal context, while Piper interprets the law-court in the context of God's glory. Yet if justification (i.e., imputation) is necessarily situated in a covenantal context, it is precisely in this way that Wright's dichotomy presents a false dilemma. Reformed theology has never argued that God's essential righteousness is transferred to believers, but that the complete fulfillment of the law by our covenant head becomes the basis for the imputation of righteousness.

So Piper's contention that the "belittling of God's glory" is the main problem of Romans 1–3 is not wrong but incomplete.[69] The "belittling of God's glory" is specifically defined in the relationship God stipulated to Adam and to Israel in the form of a covenant. Wright contends that "imputation makes no sense at all." Piper replies, "And this is because he treats the righteousness of God merely in terms of the actions of the Judge, not in terms of his deeper attribute of righteousness."[70] Piper says, "It is not a category mistake to speak of the defendant 'receiving the Judge's righteousness.' This is, in fact, what the language of justification demands in a law-court where the Judge is omniscient and just and the charge is 'none is [morally] righteous' (Rom. 3:10)."[71]

Yet both miss the point that covenant theology highlights. None of the Reformers taught that God's essential righteousness is imputed or transferred to believers. Rather, they taught that the meritorious active and passive obedience of Christ as the faithful Servant of the LORD has been imputed to believers. So if the covenantal context is too faint in Piper's construal, missing from Wright's account is the third party in the courtroom—namely, the Last Adam, who as covenant head and mediator fulfills the terms of the law-covenant and bears its sanctions on behalf of those whom he represents. Wright's objections can be properly addressed not by bracketing covenant theology but only by offering a *different* covenant theology.

Obedience and Justification

The second example is Romans 2:13, where Paul says that the doers, not just the hearers of the law, will be justified. This is the *sedes doctrinae* for Wright's conviction that there is a final justification on the basis of the believer's works. "Paul has spoken in Romans 2 about the final justification of God's people on the basis of their whole life."[72] "Present justification declares, on the basis of faith, what future justification will affirm publicly (according to 2:14–16 and 8:9–11) on the basis of the entire life."[73]

I find Piper's challenge to Wright's exegesis of Romans 2:13 entirely persuasive. Even when the Spirit is honored as the gracious source of this obedience, it nevertheless remains for Wright that believers will be justified or vindicated on the last day on the basis of their cooperation with the Spirit. For the record, this is precisely the official Roman Catholic position. It is not Pelagian, but it is also not Pauline. According to Wright, present justification is simply the acknowledgment that we belong to the covenant community and that it anticipates the final justification; yet the latter will be "on the basis of the entire life a person has led in the power of the Spirit—that is, it occurs on the basis of 'works' in Paul's redefined sense."[74] "The Spirit is the path by which Paul traces the route from justification by faith in the present to justification, by the complete life lived, in the future."[75]

I agree with Piper that "the doers of the law" in Romans 2:13 are not Christians but an empty set.[76] I would add that Wright's definition of the works of the law here stands in some contradiction to his insistence that this phrase refers exclusively to the ethnic boundary markers (i.e., ceremonies).[77] Here, at least, "justified by works of the law" is taken in the sense interpreted by the Reformers—namely, as faithfulness to all of God's commands. Yet, unfortunately, *our* obedience becomes the basis for final justification in Wright's view.

Furthermore, Wright's interpretation of Romans 2:13 simply does not fit the logic of Paul's argument, which is to challenge Jewish "boasting in the law" so that "the whole world might become guilty before God." No one is righteous, not even one. "So by the works of the law no human being will be justified in his sight, since through the law comes knowledge of sin" (3:20). Therefore, verse 28: "We hold that one is justified by faith apart from works of the law." Paul's massive transition in verse 21 makes sense only in the light of the universal condemnation of the world by the law: "But now the righteousness of God has been manifested apart from law," which Jews and Gentiles have only through faith in Christ.

However, "the doers of the law" is not quite an empty set since Jesus fulfilled all righteousness on behalf of his coheirs. So we are saved by works after all, but by Christ's rather than by our own. It is not merely verses here and there that will be persuasive on this point, but the broader exegetical conviction that Christ has assumed Adam's representative role, fulfilling all righteousness (i.e., the covenant of works) and dispensing it to his coheirs in a covenant of grace. Otherwise, Christ's active obedience is suspended in midair. In the absence of Christ's active obedience in fulfilling the covenant of works, Wright substitutes the imperfect but Spirit-led faithfulness of the believer's whole life lived.

Apostasy and Perseverance

The third example is the question of apostasy. With formulas such as "Get in by grace, stay in by obedience," covenantal nomism of various stripes has no trouble maintaining that believers can lose their salvation. However, I have argued that this rests on a conflation of the Mosaic and Abrahamic covenants, Sinai and Zion, law and gospel. The other popular alternative is to regard warnings such as we find in Hebrews 6 as merely hypothetical.

There is, however, a third answer. Affirming the unity of the covenant of grace in both testaments, Reformed theology also acknowledges the distinction between the visible and the invisible church. No less than in the Old Testament is the covenant of grace perfectly visible as the society of the elect. For now, it is a mixed body, the field in which weeds are sown among the wheat and are only separated at the final harvest.

The book of Hebrews labors the point that the new covenant is founded on better promises than the Sinai covenant, with a better mediator and a better sacrifice. With respect to the temporal promise (long life in the land), the old covenant may be characterized by the formula "Get in by grace, stay in by obedience," but the new covenant is *sola gratia* throughout. In Hebrews (especially chapters 4 and 6), however, apostasy does not seem hypothetical. People are actually in danger of falling away from grace, which is the concern of this Epistle.

With respect to this question of apostasy, three points stand out in my reading of Hebrews. 1) New covenant believers and old covenant believers belong to the same covenant of grace. They have had the same gospel proclaimed to them (4:2). 2) In both testaments, there is a distinction between visible membership and actual participation in Christ by faith. Those baptized and reared in the covenant community are heirs of the promise, even sharing in the Spirit in some sense and tasting of the powers of the age to come through the Word and Sacraments (6:4–8). Yet these blessings of visible membership do not save apart from embracing the reality in faith: namely, Christ and all his benefits (4:2; 6:7). 3) Apart from faith, these temporary blessings fall short of salvation (6:9). Covenant children today are in exactly the same situation as those in the old covenant: heirs of promise who are warned to embrace this inheritance rather than, like Esau, rejecting their birthright (12:15–17).

The covenantal context widens the horizon from a salvation reduced to individual salvation to God's wider purposes in history. There is no hard and fast division between soteriology and ecclesiology. Defined by its confessions, therefore, Reformed theology integrates the concern for individual salvation with ecclesiology, as well as God's covenantal purposes for a renewed cosmos, without forcing a false choice between them. Apart from this covenantal matrix, the Reformed understanding of justification loses many of its best arguments and falls prey to caricatures. "My anxiety about what has now been seen as *the traditional Reformed view*," Wright says, "...is that it focuses all attention on 'me and my salvation' rather than on 'God and God's purposes', which—as we see in the Gospels, and in e.g. Romans 8—are much wider than just my salvation" (emphasis added).[78] Given the way in which Reformed theology has consistently integrated covenant and eschatology with its doctrine of personal salvation, this is precisely the sort of caricature whose implausibility becomes apparent under closer scrutiny.

I have merely scratched the surface of classic covenant theology for interpreting the doctrine of justification; however, I hope at least to have made the case that the appropriate question is not *whether* covenant theology but *which* covenant theology will provide the best paradigm for interpreting not the justification of the ungodly and much else besides.

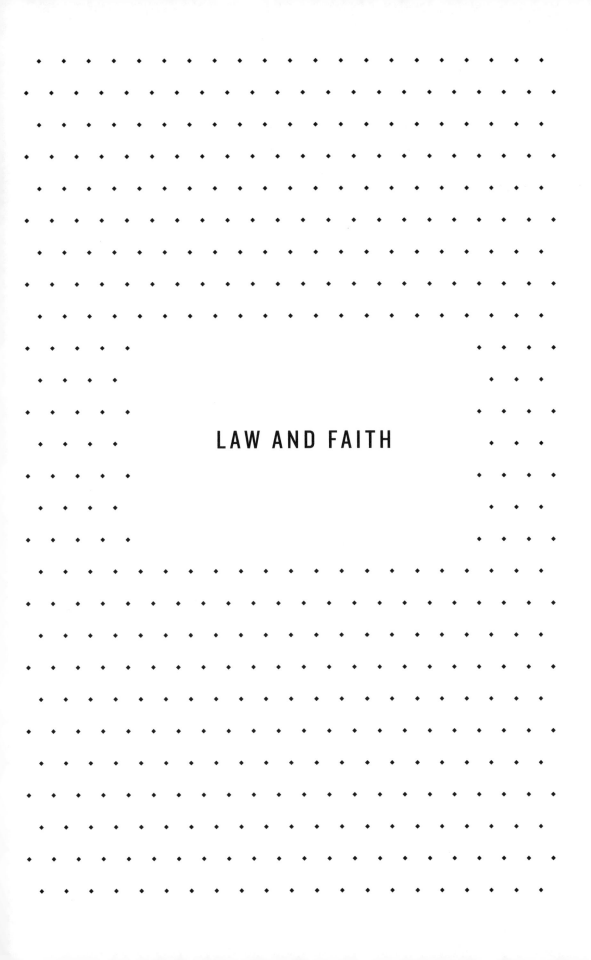

LAW AND FAITH

Confusion about the Law in Paul

BY T. DAVID GORDON

Over twenty-five years ago, I wrote my doctoral dissertation on Paul's understanding of the law. It was an old problem then, and has become problematic in new ways since then. The problem arises largely from the Pauline letters themselves—Paul sometimes speaks very favorably of the law and sometimes very unfavorably. Reconciling these positive and negative statements has been the challenge of Paul's interpreters for centuries. But other issues have arisen since Paul's day that have made the matter even more difficult. In what follows, I would like to mention four things that make it challenging to understand the law biblically.

DIFFERENT USES WITHIN THE CONFESSIONAL STANDARDS THEMSELVES

Within the Reformed confessions, "law" is used to mean two different things. Most commonly, "law" means something like "God's moral will."[1] The Westminster Confession's nineteenth chapter is entirely about God's law, and note what it says in its second section: "This law, after his fall, continued to be a *perfect rule of righteousness*; and, as such, was delivered by God upon Mount Sinai, in ten commandments, and written in two tables: the four first commandments containing our duty towards God; and the other six, our duty to man." In its sixth part, the same chapter says, "Although true believers be not under the law, as a covenant of works, to be thereby justified, or condemned; yet is it of great use to them, as well as to others; in that, as *a rule of life informing them of the will of God*, and their duty, it directs and binds them to walk accordingly." This definition of "law" in the Westminster standards is the most common definition, and it appears in many other places.[2]

In addition to this reference to "law" as God's moral will, the confessional standards use the term to mean the Sinai covenant-administration, at places such as 25:2: "The visible church, which is also catholic or universal *under the gospel* (not confined to one nation, as before *under the law*), consists of all those throughout the world that profess the true religion; and of their children: and is the kingdom of the Lord Jesus Christ, the house and family of God, out of which there is no ordinary possibility of salvation" (parentheses theirs, emphases mine). This appears to be the same usage as at 7:5: "This covenant was differently administered in the time of the law, and in the time of the gospel: *under the law,* it was administered by promises, prophecies, sacrifices, circumcision, the paschal lamb, and other types and ordinances delivered to the people of the Jews, all foresignifying Christ to come" (also 7:6 and WSC 27). In passages such as these, "law" is a synecdoche, by which that covenant-administration so characterized by law-giving is referred to by its central feature.

Perhaps most readers of the confessional literature have no difficulty with adjusting to these two definitions. It is not uncommon for words to perform multiple duties, and humans have little difficulty determining the correct meaning by context. Take the word "reformed," for instance. In the context of discussing various forms of Judaism, it means "liberal." When discussing Christian theology, it means

"Augustinian." If referring to former juvenile delinquents, it means something like "no longer spray-painting graffiti on the public high school building;" and if referring to an alcoholic it means "on the wagon." We use the same term to mean at least four different things, and we do so with no confusion. If I refer to a fellow minister in my denomination as being "Reformed," no one mistakes me to be saying anything about misguided adolescent behavior! However, if even the Westminster standards, with all their evident scholastic precision, use such an important term in more than one way, it is possible that the Scriptures do so also, and that some misunderstanding arises from this reality.

PAUL'S USE OF "THE LAW"

Adding to this possible confusion is a reality that very few recognize: Paul's use of *nomos* is the polar opposite of "law" in the confessional literature. Paul rarely, if ever, employs the term to refer to God's moral will. He ordinarily employs it as a synecdoche (a part that refers to the whole) for the Sinai covenant, as he does at Galatians 3:17: "This is what I mean: the law, which came 430 years afterward, does not annul a covenant previously ratified by God, so as to make the promise void." Note here that the "law" is something that appeared historically 430 years after the promissory covenant made with Abraham (which is designated by the synecdoche "promise"). Paul undoubtedly is reflecting here on the narrative of Exodus 12:40–41, which specifies a 430-year interval between the two covenants.

Paul did not invent this usage of *nomos* as a synecdoche for the covenant characterized by the giving of so many laws; there is evidence of this within the Greek translation of the Old Testament itself. Daniel 9:13 says this: "As it is written in the Law of Moses all this calamity has come upon us; yet we have not entreated the favor of the Lord our God, turning from our iniquities and gaining insight by your truth." The expression "Law of Moses" is a good, literal rendition of the Hebrew, *btorah mosheh*. But the Septuagint translators took a different route. Though they almost always rendered the Hebrew *Torah* with the Greek *nomos*, they did not do so here. Here they translated the Hebrew "in the Law of Moses" with the Greek "in the *covenant* of Moses."[3] Since the covenant made at Mount Sinai was so characterized by God writing laws on the "tablets of the covenant," which were later stored in the "ark of the covenant," that covenant itself could be referred to by this central feature of the revelation of so much law.

Space does not permit me here to argue that, in my judgment, *nomos* virtually always means this in the Pauline letters; to do so would require a scholarly article of its own. But suffice it to say that I concur entirely with Douglas J. Moo: "What is vital for any accurate understanding of Paul's doctrine of law is to realize that Paul uses *nomos* most often and most basically of the Mosaic law."[4] Many particular Pauline passages are routinely misunderstood when people assume that the usage in the confessional literature is the same as Paul's usage. Moo has also observed this confusion: "As we have seen, the Reformers, as most theologians today, use 'law' to mean anything that demands something of us. In this sense, 'law' is a basic factor in all human history; and man is in every age, whether in the OT or NT, confronted with 'law.' What is crucial to recognize is that this is *not* the way in which Paul usually uses the term *nomos*."[5]

Neither Moo nor I suggest that the confessional literature needs to use "law" as Paul did; we merely call attention to the confusion that results if we are not aware that the usages are different. For Paul, "law" is not the term he employs to describe God's moral will; it is the synecdoche he employs to describe the covenant God made with the Israelites at Mount Sinai, 430 years after the previous covenant was made with Abraham.

JAMES D. G. DUNN'S THESIS ABOUT "WORKS OF THE LAW"

A third and more recent confusion about the law is James D. G. Dunn's thesis that "works of the law" refers only to the *marking* laws (dietary laws, the Jewish calendar, and circumcision), rather than to the stipulations of the Mosaic covenant in their entirety.[6] For Dunn, this "solves" the problem of Paul's negative statements about the law, because, by this theory, Paul's only (or primary) problem with the law is where it demarcates the Jews as a particular social group distinct from others. Were this theory true, it would serve the purposes of the so-called New Perspectives on Paul, because one of the motivations of some of these perspectives is to improve the Jewish-Christian dialogue, especially in the post-Holocaust setting. If Paul's negative comments about the law are merely about a few particulars within the law, then Paul is not critical of Torah-centric religion, such as the one that emerges in the first century of the Common Era.

The problem with Dunn's view, attractive as it might be for ecumenical purposes, is that Paul always viewed the Mosaic Law as a single whole. Paul perceived the tablets of the covenant, and all of the other Mosaic commands, as being a body of stipulations of a particular covenant: the Israelites were obliged to keep *all* of them. Further, in at least one of the passages where the expression "works of the law" appears, Paul rather evidently indicates that anyone who is obliged to one of the stipulations of that covenant is obliged to all of them: "For all who rely on works of the law are under a curse; for it is written, 'Cursed be everyone who does not abide by *all things* written in the Book of the Law, and do them.'"[7] Paul explains the law as threatening with its curse-sanctions those who do not abide by "all things" written in the book of the law. Further, he actually *adds* this to the original text. The Greek Old Testament of Deuteronomy 27:26 simply says, "The things written in the book of the law," and Paul adds the "all" as communicating the spirit intended. Note then that Paul self-consciously supplements the actual Greek of the passage by his addition of the word "all," indicating that for him the "works of the law" include all of the things written in the book of the law, not just some of them.[8] As he said later in Galatians: "I testify again to every man who accepts circumcision that he is obligated to keep the *whole* law" (5:3).

One of the very real "problems" Paul had with the law was that it distinguished Jew and Gentile; on this point, Dunn is incontestably right. In Ephesians, he called the law a "dividing wall of hostility" (2:15). But Paul had other problems with the law that go beyond the way it distinguished Jew and Gentile. There were things the law "could not" do (Rom. 8:3)—it could not make alive (Gal. 3:21); it justified no one (Rom. 3:20); it was the "power of sin" (1 Cor. 15:56); it placed people under a threatened curse (Gal. 3:10); it brought wrath (Rom. 4:15); it increased trespasses (Rom. 5:20); it aroused our sinful passions (Rom. 7:5); it held us captive (Rom. 7:6); and it revived slumbering sin (Rom. 7:11). It is not surprising, then, that Paul referred to the ministry of Moses as a ministry of death and condemnation (2 Cor. 3:7, 9). Paul acknowledged that the law played an extremely important role in the history of redemption, but that temporary role was terminated by the work of Christ (Gal. 3:19, 23–25). For Paul, Christ terminated the law comprehensively (Rom. 10:4), not just parts of it.

We love our Jewish friends, and we often admire their fidelity to their faith, their charity toward a world that has rarely returned the favor, and the integrity of their moral lives. But, as Rabbi Neusner has himself pointed out, for two millennia since the demise of temple religion, two world religions have emerged, each tracing its roots to the temple religion of the Hebrew scriptures, but each reading those scriptures through different lenses:

> The New Testament is the prism through which the light of the Old comes to Christianity. The canon of rabbinical writings is the star that guides Jews to the revelation of Sinai, the Torah....The claim of these two great Western traditions, in all their rich variety, is for the veracity not merely of the Scriptures, but also of Scriptures as interpreted by the New Testament or the Babylonian Talmud....Both the apostles and the rabbis thus reshaped the antecedent religion of Israel, and both claimed to be Israel....For the Christian, therefore, the issue of Messiah predominated; for the rabbinic Jew, the issue of Torah; and for both, the question of salvation was crucial.[9]

As Rabbi Neusner indicated, one religion is law-centric and one is Messiah-centric. No amount of ecumenical goodwill and no truthful perspective on Paul can eradicate the significance of those differences.

THE PERVASIVENESS OF MONO-COVENANTAL TENDENCIES IN LATE TWENTIETH-CENTURY REFORMED THOUGHT

A fourth source of confusion regarding the law is due to the mono-covenantalist tendencies in the thought of many modern evangelical leaders, ranging in extremes from Daniel P. Fuller to the otherwise traditional and orthodox Reformed theologian John Murray of Westminster Theological Seminary in Philadelphia. Using the latter as an example, Murray brought a remarkable breadth of learning to everything he wrote and was in every other respect traditionally Reformed. There was, however, one area in which he candidly acknowledged his own distance from Reformed orthodoxy: "It appears to me that the covenant theology, notwithstanding the finesse of analysis with which it was worked out and the grandeur of its articulated systematization, needs recasting."[10] Later, in the same work, he wrote: "From the beginning of God's disclosures to men in terms of covenant we find a unity of conception which is to the effect that a divine covenant is a sovereign administration of grace and of promise."[11]

Murray's proposed "recasting" of covenant theology tended to see "unity" where the previous history of covenant theology had seen differences. For Murray, every biblical covenant is a "sovereign administration of grace and promise." This causes profound difficulty for the reading of Galatians, where Paul contrasts the Abrahamic and Sinai covenants in five distinct ways, using "promise" as a synecdoche for one, but "law" (*not* grace, *not* promise) to describe the other: "This is what I mean: the law, which came 430 years afterward, does not annul a covenant previously ratified by God, so as to make the promise void. For *if the inheritance comes by the law, it no longer comes by promise*; but God gave it to Abraham by a promise" (Gal. 3:17–18, emphasis mine). Paul distinguishes these covenants as not only different in *number* ("these women are *two* covenants," Gal. 4:24), but different in *kind*. If the inheritance of what was pledged to Abraham comes by the law, it no longer comes by promise. The one covenant is promissory; the other is not: "These women are two covenants. One is from Mount Sinai, bearing children for slavery; she is Hagar."[12]

But the confusion Murray introduced on this point is not restricted to understanding Galatians. His tendency to see "unity" in all biblical covenants has the effect of eroding the distinctives of each covenant, and tends to promote an expectation of continuity between covenants that was not true of the previous covenant theology tradition. Geerhardus Vos, for instance, argued that biblical theology attempted to do justice to two principles as it studied the Scriptures— continuity (he sometimes called this the "organic principle") and discontinuity (he awkwardly called this the "principle of periodicity"): "Biblical Theology, rightly defined, is nothing else than *the exhibition of the organic progress of supernatural revelation in its historic continuity and multiformity*."[13] For Vos, as biblical revelation unfolds, we observe both continuity *and* multiformity. We do not expect either one without the other, yet Murray expected to find a "unity of conception" in all biblical covenants.

John Murray cast a long shadow. His influence on Calvinistic evangelicalism and in his considerable writing was and is justifiably significant. He himself, apart from this one self-conscious area of difference from the covenant theology tradition, remained orthodox in every other way. His general tendency to see unity was tempered by his wide theological reading within the Reformed tradition and by his careful exegesis of biblical texts. But others, influenced by his general mono-covenantalist tendency, did not temper their views as he did his. Resistant to perceiving differences between the various biblical covenants,

Murray's followers (some of whom may not even be aware of his influence) have resisted the kinds of contrasts Paul observed in Galatians. Within a half-generation of Murray's death, the Reformed tradition witnessed the price to be paid for mono-covenantalism: Norman Shephard's views on justification, which resisted a strong distinction between faith and works as instruments of justification; theonomy, which resisted a distinction between the laws of the Israelite theocracy and the laws of non-theocratic states; paedo communion, which resisted the distinction between the Passover as a house meal and the Lord's Supper as an ecclesiastical meal; and the Auburn theology, which resisted many of the distinctions that once distinguished Catholics and Protestants.[14]

If we asked a typical group of Murray-influenced individuals today, "Are we under the law?" most would say "no," albeit hesitantly, but some would probably qualify the matter in some way. Paul didn't. Paul said, "You are not under law but under grace" (Rom. 6:14, 15, cf. Gal. 5:4). Note how starkly Paul contrasts the Mosaic covenant with our own:

> For the letter *kills*, but the Spirit gives *life*. Now if the *ministry of death*, carved in letters on stone, came with such glory that the Israelites could not gaze at Moses' face because of its glory, which was being brought to an end, will not the *ministry of the Spirit* have even more glory? For if there was glory in the ministry of *condemnation*, the ministry of *righteousness* must far exceed it in glory. (2 Cor. 3:6–9)

This last confusion is actually related to the first. If we think "law" means God's moral will, then Paul's negative statements must be statements about some alleged first-century abuse of the law, because surely Paul would not find fault with God's moral will. But if, for Paul, "law" refers to the temporary (and frightening) covenant God made with the Israelites at Sinai, a covenant that threatened (and later brought) curse-sanctions for disobedience, a covenant under which many Israelites died—whether from snakes, Assyrians or Babylonians—then we are able to understand why his comments about it are often so negative. Jeremiah, living under the Sinai covenant, looked forward to the day when God would make "a new covenant with the house of Israel and the house of Judah, *not like* the covenant that I made with their fathers" (Jer. 31:31–32). Paul, as a minister of this "not like" covenant, did not hesitate to distinguish law and grace (Rom. 4:16, 6:14, Gal. 2:21, 5:4), law and faith (Rom. 4:13–16; Gal. 2:16, 3:2, 5, 12; Phil. 3:9), or law and Christ (Rom. 7:4, 10:4; Gal. 2:21, 3:24, 5:4, Phil. 3:9).

CONCLUSION

Law is one of the more significant realities to be dealt with in Scripture. It is not surprising, therefore, that there has not been universal consensus on how to understand it. But if we can evade/avoid the four confusions that have appeared both less recently and more recently, perhaps our degree of unity will increase.

CHAPTER 03

The Justification of the Guilty, Not the Righteous

BY MICHAEL S. HORTON

I n an *America* article,[1] English professor Brian Abel Ragen, a lay Roman Catholic, observes that a good number of Protestant hymns have made their way into the Mass. He laments not only that the "reforms" since the 1960s have produced a rash of tacky imitation pop music, but that the older Protestant hymns themselves have been revised. These hymns haven't been changed by Catholics because of their Protestant theology, but because of a force that appears greater than either tradition: modernity. "Amazing Grace," Ragen points out, now reads, "Amazing grace! How sweet the sound! That *saved and strengthened* me!" Readers will recall the original line as, "That saved *a wretch like* me!" Ragen observes of the classic hymn's author,

> While Newton believed that human beings were wretches, in desperate need of a savior, these 20th-century adapters clearly believe that they and the congregations who sing their words are perfectly nice people—almost nice enough to be Unitarians. They are not bad—certainly not *wretches*; they have simply lost their way. They are not wicked; they merely have a handicap—a dysfunction—from which they hope to recover.

However, this misses the whole point, Ragen insists. "Grace is amazing because it saves *wretches*, not because it puts a final polish on nice people." After all, "You cannot be saved if you are not lost. You cannot be redeemed if you are not in hock. You cannot be freed unless you are enslaved." While rejecting human sinfulness, the churches want to retain some sentimental notion of redemption, Ragen says. "Probably the worst example," in his opinion, is "'And They'll Know We Are Christians by Our Love.'" Our contemporary praise music, sung in both evangelical and Roman Catholic churches, has left out sin and grace as categories, instead praising ourselves for our love and devotion. Ragen's conclusion is undeniable:

> Those who actually believe in the doctrines of Christianity will view with alarm a movement through which the church itself undermines its basic doctrines. They will be saddened to sing bad poetry, when they could sing good poetry. Even more, they will be appalled to see their own hymns weakening the one Christian doctrine that can be verified from the television news, from the behavior of their colleagues—and themselves—at work and from the quarrels over their dinner-tables: human depravity. What sets Christianity apart from the rest of the world's religions is that Christians both recognize a Fall and proclaim a Savior. They will know we are Christians, not by our love, but by our recognition that we are worms and wretches.

One of the marvelous things about a public confession of sin in the liturgy is that you have to say it even when you don't want to. I can't recall the last time I went into the service longing to agree with God that I am "a miserable offender" who is "not worthy to gather up the crumbs under the table" of God's grace. But it is a testimony to the power of the law and the gospel that when I do say this, and receive God's forgiveness, I know why I am a Christian again.

Sentimentalism has created an alternative to Christianity, even when it goes by the latter's name. Writing just after the Second World War, Harry Blamires (a close friend of C. S. Lewis) wrote,

> A curse of contemporary Christendom has been the replacement of traditional theology by a new system which we may call *Twentieth-century Sentimental Theology. Sentimental Theology* has invented a God: it insists that he is a God of love, and implies that it is therefore his eternal concern that a thumping good time should be had by all. Are we in the dumps? Pray to this God, and, at a word, he restores us to self-confident buoyancy....Five minutes of prayer to this many-sided God, and we shall be able to rejoice indiscriminately with sinner and saint; we shall be able to spread the family spirit of Christian charity like a blanket over every disloyalty and infidelity conceived in Hell and planted in men's hearts. So runs the Sentimental Creed.[2]

Why is it so hard for us to believe that God *cannot* acquit the guilty, that he cannot love even if it means that perfect justice is not done? To understand that, we need to contrast the sentimental creed (Love Is God) with the Christian creed (God Is Love).

LOVE IS GOD: THE AMERICAN RELIGION

As early as the turn of the twentieth century, philosopher William James was providing Americans with a philosophical theory that had already been taken for granted in the democratic experience. As the father of "pragmatism," James argued that there is no such thing as truth in terms of an absolute fact "out there." Rather, truth was to be made and remade, judged in terms of its results—or, as he put it, in terms of "its cash-value in experiential terms." In more recent times, philosopher Richard Rorty has carried this view forward, arguing for the notion of "truth" as "therapy." Ironists such as Rorty believe that what we call "truths" are simply coping mechanisms. If they serve some therapeutic benefit, so much the better. What is interesting, though, is that this reign of therapeutic well-being is nearly universal in our culture. I once read a newspaper article on the "Toronto Blessing" in which a well-known secular psychologist gave the movement his own blessing by acknowledging likely therapeutic benefits. Similarly, Pat Robertson has argued repeatedly that Christianity must be true because medical statistics show that people who pray and belong to a "faith community" are healthier.

Whether it's Richard Gere singing the praises of Buddhist spirituality or evangelicals offering their testimonies, therapeutic results fetch a high price. Thus we are told that making people feel guilty is the very thing we should avoid. A steady parade of TV talk shows, small groups, popular books, tapes, and radio broadcasts—both secular and religious—insist on it.

From the outset, we should acknowledge that there is such a thing as bad guilt.[3]

But even though we have suppressed guilt, denied guilt in specific instances, rationalized and exploited it, rarely if ever has an entire culture banished it altogether. When guilt goes, it is no longer possible to treat people as responsible agents. They become victims instead.

We see this, of course, in our treatment of criminals in the justice system. (In actuality, much of it could be called the *therapeutic* system.) While we should avoid careless generalizations that fail to appreciate the positive effect of reformatory justice, what is both obvious and ominous is the triumph of the principle that the criminal is not, *prima facie*, responsible for his or her actions. Victims of dysfunctional backgrounds, they are broken selves that need mending. Their condition is medical, not innate, and their antisocial behavior is not really a sign of wickedness but of illness. They are not "whole." Thus the primary purpose of criminal justice is to reform these fractured selves and restore them to wholeness. Lacking standards of good and evil, the only counterweights are "victims' rights" coalitions. Even there, it is not justice, but the offended party's rights, that obtains center stage. In that scenario, revenge easily supplants justice.

What does all of this have to do with our understanding of guilt in the Christian faith? Plenty. While it is true that the Bible describes us both in terms of sinners and those who are sinned against, victimizers and victims, neither "wholeness" nor "revenge" can substitute for justice. Guilt is to justice what wholeness is to criminal reform and revenge is to victim's rights. While the cross is always foolishness to those who are perishing, its "foolishness" is particularly acute in a therapeutic age. Note, for instance, the rationale one contemporary theologian offers for rejecting the classic Christian statement of the problem and its solution:

> Is it not a slightly odd view of a morally perfect God that the divine nature can be so slighted and offended by what human beings do?...Anselm's idea is that the penalty must be paid in full; but is this really compatible with belief in the mercy of God? Secondly, even if one can accept that the sinner must pay such a tremendous penalty, how can it be just for someone else to pay it for me? ... God shows love by healing, forgiving, suffering for us. God gives us love by placing his Spirit in our hearts. God places before us the ideal of the Christ life, and forms it within us as we contemplate it. But there is here no substitutionary death, no vicarious justice, no literal death of one person in place of another.[4]

Charles Finney and a host of other American revivalists have shared this perspective. Today many evangelicals implicitly share the view offered above by Oxford theologian Keith Ward: salvation equals "healing, forgiving, [and] suffering" love. Such love comes to us as a result of God "placing his Spirit in our hearts" and placing "before us the ideal of the Christ life," forming it "within us as we contemplate it." Guilt does not even have to be denied, so long as it is soft-peddled or ignored.

Hardly anyone can object to this kind of "salvation," because it is the solution to an utterly inoffensive problem. What sense does a substitutionary, vicarious, propitiatory sacrifice of a God-Man make if the problem is something other than guilt? People can even go on believing in the existence of hell, as 85 percent of American adults do, while barely 11 percent fear the possibility of going there. We are good people who could be better. And even when we are bad, it's something we do, not something we are. Either we're too nice or God's too nice, or maybe both. But guilt is not on the top of our agenda.

In 1996, the Church of England made news by announcing that there is no such thing as eternal damnation, calling the doctrine "a distortion of the revelation of God's love." Yet this is the direction of much of popular evangelical reflection these days as well. The bottom line is that we want God to love unjustly. Or let me rephrase that: we want God to love us and other nice people like us unjustly. But God cannot love in this manner. He cannot love at the expense of everything else. He cannot deny his total character in order to express any single attribute. God loves justly and shows mercy righteously. He is both "just and the justifier of the ungodly."

GOD IS LOVE: THE BIBLICAL RELIGION

An essential mark of God's nature is what theologians call "simplicity." As seventeenth-century theologian Francis Turretin describes it, "The simplicity of God...is his incommunicable attribute by which the divine nature is conceived by us not only as free from all composition and division, but also as incapable of composition and divisibility." The Westminster divines put it in these terms: God is "without parts or passions." In other words, he is not made up of components: "I Am Who I Am." For God, essence and existence are one and the same. This means that he cannot love unjustly any more than he can condemn unjustly. He cannot lie in pursuit of the truth or violate his holiness in order to express his goodness. He is what he is *simultaneously*, each attribute participating in a unity—not a unity that "makes up" God, but that is God.

After Israel's idolatry at Mount Sinai, Moses intercedes and God agrees to maintain his presence among his people. Moses cut new tablets of stone and, according to God's command, met God on top of the mountain. There God proclaimed his name again: "The Lord, the Lord God, merciful and gracious, long-suffering, and abounding in goodness and truth, keeping mercy for thousands, forgiving iniquity and transgression and sin, by no means clearing the guilty, visiting the iniquity of the fathers upon the children and the children's children to the third and the fourth generation" (Exod. 34:6–7). Note that God is only God as he is all of this together: merciful and gracious, just and "by no means clearing the guilty." In fact, God's justice descends upon the children and the children's children. God's nature hardly satisfies the contemporary appeal of therapeutic well-being: "God is jealous, and the Lord avenges; the Lord avenges and is furious. The Lord...will not at all acquit the wicked" (Nah. 1:2–3). "I cannot endure iniquity" (Isa. 1:13). The issue is who God is and what he requires. That establishes who we are and what we need. We cannot start with ourselves in this matter, for our great problem is not that we are victims of dysfunction, but that we stand before an affronted God.

In the worse moments of our history, there has been a tendency to make it sound as if God had simply gotten up on the wrong side of the bed. A sort of cranky old man who is always worried about the neighborhood kids running through his flowerbed. This is the sort of picture that some forms of preaching offered in past generations. But throughout the story of God's people, nothing is more apparent than their treachery and God's patience. Hardly "trigger-happy," God restrains his wrath. But he will not, for he cannot, let injustice reign. While that has always been bad news for oppressors, it has given hope to the oppressed. The problem is, none of us thinks he or she belongs to the former number.

HOW GOD LOVES THE GUILTY

If God cannot acquit the guilty or endure sin, how can he also love us? If we do not finally arrive at that dilemma, we know nothing of the story we find in the Bible. Throughout history, the question, "How does God love the guilty?" has been answered in various ways. Some say he loves the guilty by simply "letting bygones be bygones." God writes up the ticket, but never turns it in. Others say that this sacrifices too much. Rather, God loves the guilty by making them less guilty. By reforming their character and redeeming their past, he heals them and makes them lovable. Neither of these options matches the biblical response, however. The apostle Paul explains how God loves the guilty:

> Now we know that whatever the law says, it says to those who are under the law, so that every mouth may be silenced and the whole world held accountable to God. Therefore no one will be declared righteous in his sight by observing the law; rather, through the law we become conscious of sin. But now a righteousness from God, apart from law, has been made known, to which the Law and the Prophets testify. (Rom. 3:19–21)

First, says the apostle, there are two kinds of righteousness. Both are of the same quality: perfect conformity to God's holy character and moral will. But "the righteousness that is by the Law" is the righteousness of God (v. 21). It is synonymous with God's personal character: "Your eyes are too pure to look on evil; you *cannot* tolerate wrong" (Hab. 1:13). "The arrogant cannot stand in your presence. You hate all who do wrong" (Ps. 5:5). The law is not external to God, but is the revelation of his very person. He is not by nature angry, but he is by nature just, righteous, holy, and true. Thus he is capable of anger when his character is violated.

Furthermore, God is not only righteous in himself, but because this is his universe, he requires righteousness: "For I say unto you, That except your righteousness exceed the righteousness of the scribes and Pharisees, you shall in no case enter the kingdom of heaven" (Matt. 5:20). "Who shall ascend to the hill of the Lord? or who shall stand in his holy place? He who has clean hands and a pure heart" (Ps. 24:3). That God "looks on the heart" does not come as good news to those with guilty hearts (Jer. 17:9).[5]

When Jesus appears, he heightens the perfection required in the law. Whereas the Pharisees thought they had kept God's commands if they had not externally violated it, Jesus reminded them that the law required an internal perfection of which they fell far short. God's righteous nature and righteous requirement leads, when it is violated, to a righteous verdict, as Paul explains in the first two chapters of Romans. As people reject all knowledge of God and truth, they descend into the deepest debauchery and incur an ever-increasing judgment. But lest the Jews—or, for that matter, today's Christians—boast in their possession of the law, Paul reminds us that we are all equally condemned (Rom. 2:1–6, 17–24). Those who proudly tout "Judeo-Christian values" are in no better position before God than the advocates of secularism and perversion. Jesus makes the same point in his parable of the Pharisee and the publican.

The law condemns, Paul concludes (Rom. 3:5–18). It offers no way out, no possibility of time off for good behavior. God's justice is incapable of flexibility or accommodation because he would be less than God if he were to "bend the rules." As nineteenth-century Princeton theologian Charles Hodge reminds us in his *Commentary on Romans*:

> This is the office of the Law. It was not designed to give life, but so to convince of sin that men may be led to renounce their own righteousness and trust in the righteousness of Christ as the only and all-sufficient ground of their acceptance with God….The office of the Law is neither to justify nor to sanctify. It convinces and condemns. All efforts to secure the favour of God, therefore, by obedience must be vain.

The law is everything, from Genesis to Revelation, that reveals both God's righteous character and his will for our lives—whether the Ten Commandments, the fruit of the Spirit, the Sermon on the Mount, or any other command or exhortation in Scripture. Our nature is to believe in ourselves, and our culture accentuates this heresy, so when we hear a command or an exhortation, our immediate response is, "I can do that." We are like the plumber who took a look at Niagara Falls and shouted, "Just give me a minute. I can fix it." We call the Bible, "God's road map for life," or "The Owner's Manual," but this is to say that the Bible is all law. When churches are impatient with theology and demand "more application," they are often simply caving in to our natural gravitation toward self-help and away from the cross.

Paul, however, says that the purpose of the law in this matter of finding peace with God is not to encourage us but to discourage us, so that we will find ourselves condemned and flee to Christ for safety: "Because no one will be declared righteous in his sight by observing the law; rather, through the law we become conscious of sin." Thus the explanation that God loves the guilty by merely reforming them is ruled out entirely.

"Law" can appear as rationalism: If I just know all the right facts. It can appear as moralism: If I just do the right things. It can appear as emotionalism: If I just have the right feelings. It can appear as sentimentalism: If I just love. This last one was John Wesley's suggestion. "Perfectionism" had to do not with actions ("mistakes," as he called them), but with the entire sanctification of the heart so that one loved perfectly. But Jesus tells us that love is the *summary* of the law! One cannot be perfect in heart or in love if one continues to sin against God or one's neighbor.

There is hope, though—the hope that freed a guilt-ridden Martin Luther. Let us look back to the second of the two kinds of righteousness Paul contrasts: "But now a righteousness *from* God, apart from law, has been made known, to which the Law and the Prophets testify" (v. 21). If the righteousness that is by law announces that which God *is*, the righteousness that is by faith announces that which God *gives*. The law and the gospel, on the point of justification, are completely contradictory. The law commands, with no offers of mercy; the gospel gives, with no threats of judgment. Both alternatives to this way of God loving the guilty find this answer perfectly scandalous. Neither the sentimentalist nor the moralist can abide the thought that God actually saves and loves the guilty *as* guilty. But this is exactly what Paul is saying: the law rewards those who are perfectly righteous with eternal life; the gospel freely gives those who are wicked eternal life, even though they are still wicked. Paul announces: "But to him who does not work but believes on him who justifies the ungodly, his faith is accounted for righteousness, just as David also describes the blessedness of the man to whom God imputes righteousness apart from works" (Rom. 4:5–6).

This message has been the scandal of Christianity from the beginning. The Pharisees were offended, the Judaizers were put off by it, Rome anathematized it, and liberal Protestantism scorns it. How can God legally accept a person as already perfectly righteous even though that person continues to sin? Here in Romans 4:1–5, Paul leaves no question. First, this acceptance is granted to a particular sort of person: "To the person who does not work." Every religious impulse of our fallen heart insists that those who do the right thing will be paid for their labors. But, Paul counters, the gospel is nothing like that. In fact, "Now to him who works, the wages are not counted as a gift but as a debt" (Rom. 4:4). God will not give anything as a debt, but only as an undeserved gift (Rom. 11:35). All works are hereby excluded, whether of our hands or our heart. Nothing that is produced in us or by us is the gospel, and this even includes that which *God* does within us. Not the new birth, not conversion, not deciding to follow Jesus or surrendering all. For in this life, none of us perfectly follows Jesus or surrenders a great deal, much less *all*. Even our marvelous growth in sanctification is insufficient as an anchor, as it is never a perfect righteousness in this life. Our imperfect sanctification could condemn us as surely as unbelief and rebellion. "Our *righteousness* is as filthy rags" (Isa. 64:6). We need a perfect righteousness, so it cannot be the product of our own head, hands, or heart. It must be an "alien righteousness," something put on us. In the words of the hymn "Rock of Ages":

> Not the labors of my hands
> can fulfill thy law's commands;
> could my zeal no respite know,
> could my tears forever flow,
> all for sin could not atone;
> thou must save, and thou alone.

The person whom God "declares righteous" does not work for it; instead, he "trusts God who justifies the wicked." It is not just any kind of trusting, or even trusting in God, that saves. We are justified only by trusting in God's promise to justify us as wicked sinners. Not even our faith justifies, but is the empty hand that receives God's gift, and this faith is as much a gift as justification itself. Trusting God "who justifies the wicked" is far more difficult than trusting God who justifies those who are good. It is like someone taking a demolition ball and knocking down the stilts that prop up our religious psyche. It takes everything away from us in order to give us so much more than we could ever have expected (Phil. 3:3–10).

Paul's word in Romans 4 for "justify" (*dikaio*) does not mean "to make righteous," but "to declare righteous." Nor does it mean merely "to pardon." A criminal who is pardoned by the governor is nevertheless not said to be justified. If you are a criminal, it is easy to trust a judge who acquits criminals. That simply means he is lenient. But God does not (for he cannot) acquit criminals. Instead, he *justifies* them. He does not let them go even though he still considers them guilty; he declares them righteous, so that as far as justice is concerned, they have perfectly satisfied all requirements of the law. But God only justifies the wicked. He does not justify the righteous.

At the end of it all, God's saving work in Christ serves "to demonstrate at the present time [God's] righteousness, that he might be just and the justifier of the one who has faith in Jesus" (Rom. 3:26). As the hymn writer Augustus Toplady put it, "Nothing in my hands I bring, simply to Thy cross I cling." We never leave justification in order to move on to the "higher ground" of sanctification. The cross and resurrection of Christ are never a grammar school from which we graduate, but form the only possible wellspring of both declarative and progressive holiness.

Thus God does not acquit the wicked. Nor does he love us "just as we are," nor even in view of what he will make of us one day, but only as we are "in Christ." He does not—cannot—simply "let bygones be bygones." Instead, he does something much greater: he justifies the wicked. He actually declares them to be something they are not within their own hearts and lives. God loves his Son unconditionally, and in the Son so too are we loved. Draped in the blood-bought righteousness of the Lamb of God, we are far more than "let off" by divine carelessness; we are joint-heirs with Christ in all that he possesses. From this fountain of every blessing we are given not only the freedom from the *guilt* of our sins, but from the terrible *bondage* of our sins, so that we may be moved by divine mercy from guilt to grace to gratitude. In the comforting words of C. S. Lewis, "Though our feelings come and go, His love for us does not. It is not wearied by our sins, or our indifference; and, therefore, it is quite relentless in its determination that we shall be cured of those sins, at whatever cost to us, at whatever cost to Him."

Does Faith Mean Faithfulness?

BY SIMON GATHERCOLE

With all the controversy that has raged about justification in the past generation, it is surprising that for some time the question of what faith is has remained more marginal. This issue, however, has recently come into the foreground of both the church's and the academy's attention. This essay aims to do justice to both Paul and James, and to clarify that faith is not itself righteousness but should be regarded as trust in Christ, which also has specific verbal content. It is also not an entity, however, that can ever be isolated in the Christian life from obedience, even though faith and obedience are not to be confused.

"FAITH RECKONED AS RIGHTEOUSNESS" IN PAUL

As far as the interpretation of Paul is concerned, it is vital to recognize that God does not reckon righteousness to us on the basis of anything that we do in and of ourselves. One of the chief transformations that took place in Paul's conversion was in his understanding of sin: he came to see the true depravity of the human condition, that "the mind of the flesh is hostile to God; it does not submit to the Law of God, nor can it do so" (Rom. 8:7). This is in stark contrast to the understanding he probably would have had as a Pharisee: that despite the internal struggle of the good impulse against the evil impulse, it was both necessary and possible to choose the good. After his conversion, he realized (we do not know exactly how and when) that only by Christ's atoning work and the power of the Spirit are new life and true obedience possible.

Much of our attention here will be focused on Romans 4, which is one of the key chapters in the Bible on faith. The chapter is also taken up with a discussion of Abraham and how Paul brings the patriarch as a key witness to his doctrine of justification by faith. Here the apostle is battling against the Jewish tradition of explaining Abraham as a model of piety and (in some cases) law-observance even before the law was given. The trials of Abraham, such as the offering of Isaac on Mount Moriah, are seen in Jewish exegesis as the basis for his justification:

> Abraham was a great father of many nations, and no-one was found like him in glory, who kept the Law of the Most High, and entered into covenant with Him, and established the covenant in his flesh, and *was found faithful* in testing. (Sirach 44:19–20)

> This is the tenth trial with which Abraham was tried, and *he was found faithful*, controlled of spirit. [He begged for a place for burial in the land] because he was found faithful and he was recorded as a friend of the Lord in the heavenly tablets. (Jubilees 19:8–9; cf. 23:9–10)

> Abraham did not walk in it (sc. evil), and he was reckoned a friend of God *because he kept the commandments of God* and did not choose his own will. (Damascus Document 3:2–4)

Was not Abraham *found faithful in temptation* and it was reckoned to him as righteousness? (1 Maccabees 2:52)

The clearest statement, then, of what Paul is opposing comes in this final statement from ¹ Maccabees, although the language of being "reckoned as a friend of God" or "recorded as a friend of God" in the other two examples is very similar to that of being "reckoned as righteous." In short, in this Jewish tradition, Genesis 15:6 ("He believed the Lord and it was credited to him as righteousness") is fused together with Genesis 26:4b–5: "And in your offspring all the nations of the earth shall be blessed, because Abraham obeyed my voice *and kept my charge, my commandments, my statutes and my laws*." Thus, Abraham is reckoned righteous because of his obedience to the commandments of God; here, faith clearly is faithfulness.

Paul, on the other hand, considers that no one is righteous, not even Abraham: "For if Abraham was justified by works, then he has a boast. But not before God! For what does the Scripture say? 'Abraham believed God and it was reckoned to him as righteousness'" (Rom. 4:2–3).

Abraham, then, was not reckoned righteous in the same way that the Jewish expository tradition promoted. It is highly instructive that Paul explains the term "justify" by the phrase "reckon as righteous." In itself, this language is standard enough. But it is Paul's new understanding of this latter phrase that makes all the difference and sets him apart from the traditional Jewish understanding of Abraham. "Righteousness," in biblical terms, refers to "that which God requires" or "doing what God requires." In the view of Paul's opponents, God's justification of, or reckoning of righteousness to, Abraham was an entirely appropriate response to Abraham's faithful activity. Justification was effectively a comment on Abraham's behavior—that he had carried out what God had required of him. In Paul's view, however, God's word of justification is in opposition to what Abraham had actually done and been. For Paul, reckoning righteousness takes place when that righteousness is not there, rather than when it is there. Even though Abraham had not done what God required, it was reckoned to him as though he had. This is the thought underlying the two alternatives in Romans 4:4–5. There are two possible definitions of the term "reckon": reckoning as an obligation as per the Jewish tradition, and reckoning as a gift by which Paul clearly refers to his own view. It is not that Judaism was devoid of grace. But what does concern Paul is that justification is the gift of righteousness despite the fact that we have not done what God requires, rather than God's appropriate response to obedience. This comes about through Christ's death on the cross, although unfortunately there is not space to expound this here. What is clear, however, is that Paul views "believing God" in Romans 4:2 as different from Abraham's faithfulness in any trials he may have gone through.

A crucial question emerges, however. Is it not simply the case that "faith" is actually righteousness? This has been suggested by Robert Gundry and has provoked a certain amount of controversy. The problem with this view seems to me to be that it does not take account of Paul's subsequent arguments in Romans 4: the experience of David and the nature of God's action. The example of David again clarifies the fact that God's act of justification is a justification despite who David is. Furthermore, particularly important are the statements throughout chapter 4 about who God is. In each case, Paul makes it clear that it is part of who God is that he does not interact with the world on a tit-for-tat basis. The examples that Paul provides are of new creation and resurrection: giving life to the dead, and creating the things that are from that which is not (4:17). This kind of activity finds its climax in the resurrection of Jesus from the dead (4:24). But Paul has also included justification by faith as the first item in this sequence, in 4:5. Each of these statements in chapter 4 has a kind of "definition" of God: "The one who justifies the ungodly" (4:5); "the one who gives life to the dead and calls non-beings into being" (4:17); and "the one who raised Jesus from the dead" (4:24).

To return to the original question, then: Is the "reckoning" a reckoning of what is there, or a reckoning of what is not there? The answer seems clear on the basis of Romans 4. When God reckons a person righteous, it is despite what they are—it is not because faith is righteousness.

FAITH DETERMINED BY GOD'S ACTION

If faith is not righteousness, then what is it? Crucial here is that "faith" cannot be taken simply to be a generalized religious attitude or action that is simply given specific content in various different religions. There is no universal religious trust into which Allah, or Jesus, or the fairies at the bottom of the garden can be slotted. Paul makes it clear that the structure of faith itself is determined by who God is and how he has acted in Christ. Although "B.C.," Abraham is the classic exemplar here. The essence of faith for Paul is that it is "resurrection faith." The reason Abraham is a type of Christian faith is because he realizes he has no capacity in himself to bring about God's will; such a result can come about only by God's unilateral action of resurrection:

> He (Abraham), against hope, in hope believed that he would become the father of many nations, as was said, "So shall your offspring be." And he did not weaken in faith, but observed that his body was dead—as it was about a hundred years old—and that Sarah's womb was dead. He did not doubt the promise of God in unbelief, but was strengthened in his faith, giving glory to God, and was fully convinced that He was able to do what he had promised. (Rom. 4:18–21)

The key aspect of Abraham's faith here is that it responds to divine action and anticipates divine action. As I have argued elsewhere, Abraham's faith has two components. The first is observation of reality, namely, that Abraham must observe that his own body was as good as dead. The second is emphatically not the observation of Abraham's surroundings, but consists in his acknowledgement that God has the power to do what he has promised, despite the appearance of circumstances. As a result, the nature of faith clearly mirrors the nature of the way God acts in the world. Although Abraham's faith is a type of Christian faith, and thus not identical with it, the continuity lies in the fact that the structure—as outlined above—remains the same: it acknowledges that we are dead and yet trusts in God to give life. The fact that Abraham's faith is an Old Testament witness to Christian faith, however, means that there is a further element to be explicated—that it is faith in Christ.

FAITH IN CHRIST

Discussion of faith as "faith in Christ," however, immediately plunges us into one of the most hotly debated points in New Testament scholarship: the question of whether the phrase conventionally translated as "faith in Christ" (in Greek, *pistis Christou*) should actually be translated as "the faithfulness of Christ." The cash value of this is that some of the crucial Pauline texts on justification end up having a very different feel to them. "We know that a person is justified not by works of the Law, but only by faith in Christ" (Gal. 2:16) instead would become "We know that a person is justified not by works of the Law but only by the faithfulness of Christ." The focus shifts from trust in Christ to the actual activity of the earthly Jesus, whereby he lived the perfect life of conformity with God's will, which eventually culminated in his death. Linguistically, the translation could go either way, and so the position has to be decided on the basis of context and theology. It is a strange debate, however, because it does not divide down conventional "party lines." True, traditional scholars tend to be suspicious of the new translation. But key supporters of the "New Perspective" on Paul, such as James D. G. Dunn, also resist it. And some champion the new translation of "faithfulness of Christ" on the grounds that the traditional option makes salvation dependent on the human action of faith, while the alternative grounds it in God's action in Christ. As a result, the new reading has been favored by those influenced by Karl Barth, such as T. F. Torrance, Richard Hays, and Douglas Campbell.

I will simply select three examples of arguments made in support. One that has been particularly influential is J. W. van Henten's argument for seeing "the faith of Christ" against a Jewish martyrdom background. He argues that the combination of "faith," "blood," and "atonement" found in Romans 3:25 is most prominent in three passages in Jewish literature where a martyr is faithful to death, hence the reference in Romans to the faithfulness of Jesus.[1] On closer examination, however, it becomes clear that in fact none of the three places contain the word for faith or faithfulness!

Those who espouse the "faith of Christ" translation also often argue that it makes sense of passages that otherwise are peculiar. However, there are many more difficulties with interpreting passages where the new translation is adopted. For example, according to Richard Hays, "those of faith" (Gal. 3:7) refers to "those who are given life on the basis of [Christ's] faith." But the phrase is "capable of sustaining several interpretations," and Hays would not want to exclude the meaning of "those who believe" either. Hays grounds this in Paul's poetic way of using language, and the "multivalent and metaphorical" character of that language. The argument here becomes rather vague, in my view: while it is, of course, possible that Paul uses such a phrase in an ambiguous way, one is tempted to apply Occam's razor when there is no exegetical benefit.

The argument made by others that "justification by [human] faith" makes faith into a work has little force, especially if one considers faith as also a gift of God, as per Ephesians 2:8. In any case, it is not that God makes the Christian fit for justification by the gift of faith, since the gifts of faith and justification are simultaneous rather than chronologically sequential. None of these arguments, then, should be regarded as an obstacle to the view that faith is "faith in Christ," rather than simply a generic trust in God common to Abraham, Christ, and ourselves.

"FAITH MADE PERFECT BY WORKS" (JAMES 2:22)

As Paul and numerous theologians after him recognized, to define justification as coming by faith has its dangers. Definitions are, of course, no less true for being dangerous. In this respect, the Epistle of James has often functioned as a foil to prevent an extreme reading of Paul. This is not only true at the canonical level, but it is also an historical probability that James is in fact in dialogue with an interlocutor who reflects real-life extremist Paulines. Just as we know of Hymenaeus and Philetus who apparently took Paul's realized resurrection-eschatology (in, e.g., Eph. 2:4–7) to an extreme, and thus "departed from the truth" (2 Tim. 2:18), so also it is likely that there are those who took Paul's soteriology in an antinomian direction. Certainly some of Paul's Jewish opponents understood Paul this way (Rom. 3:8).

In this respect, James's statement that "faith works together with works" (James 2:12) is a vital pastoral demand. In fact, the Paul-James contrast is misconceived at this point, since Paul himself has an extremely strong emphasis on obedience. He talks of his goal as not merely bringing the Gentiles to come to faith in Christ, but actually to bring about "the obedience of [i.e., *that stems from*] faith" among the nations (Rom. 1:5; cf. 16:26). Paul and James both stress the necessity of obedience, without ever confusing "faith" and "obedience." Even in James, the two are not identified with one another.

Nevertheless, James's argument is distinctive and gives us a helpful perspective alongside that of Paul. (One could also have included discussion of Hebrews and the Gospels, but this must be omitted for the sake of brevity.) James's argument about faith begins in 2:14, at least as far as the specific term for "faith" (*pistis*) is concerned. That this is no idle theologizing is evident from the fact that final salvation is at stake. The immediately preceding context is that of judgment (2:12–13), and James's questions are precisely "What is the use of such faith [without works]?" and "Can such faith save?" (2:14).

The contrast between the Pauline language and that of James is very striking. The commentators conventionally set out the parallel statements as follows:

James 2:24: A person is justified by works and not by faith alone.

Romans 3:28: A person is justified by faith and not by works of the law.

Here, then, there is a pointed contrast—a contrast even more striking if one compares James with Paul (as translated by Luther) where justification is "only by faith." By contrast to Luther's exacerbation of the contrast, some modern commentators on Paul have attempted more of a *rapprochement*. J. Jeremias attempted this not least by contrasting the understandings of works in Paul and James. For Jeremias, Paul was referring to works done in obedience to the law in a legalistic fashion, whereas James means visiting the sick, caring for orphans, and such.[2] D. J. Moo, picking up on another element of Jeremias's argument, focuses on the way in which "justification" in Paul refers to initial acceptance by God and in James to final vindication at the Judgment.[3]

Our concern here, however, is merely with the question of "faith." The key is that faith does, of course, have specific content. Abraham believes "according to what was said," that "so shall your offspring be" (Rom. 4:18). Nevertheless, this content never means that faith is simply possessed, as if faith were merely an inert entity that could be regarded in isolation. In Paul's argument, it has an immediate corollary in Abraham's action. Abraham is not merely a passive recipient of faith; rather, as divine action embraces human action, Abraham is strengthened in his faith and gives glory to God (Rom. 4:20). The main danger that James sees is that to talk of "faith alone" is in danger of encouraging a focus on faith itself. The fact that Paul and James have different emphases means that our talk of faith must always be bounded by the whole of the New Testament (which has a fundamental unity and harmony), and should not simply follow Pauline categories.

That "faith is made perfect by works" is not, of course, Paul's principal concern. As we noted, his concern is to decouple "faith" from obedience to the law, from obedience in one's own power. Paul's emphasis is on the fact that obedience to the law did not lead to God's deliverance of Israel; rather, the history of the Old Testament was characterized by the repeated cycle of disobedience and judgment. James, on the other hand, is concerned with the fact that faith is something exercised. James would not dispute that this takes place in the Christian context of the new age: God gave Christians new birth by the Word, and so the church is the firstfruits of the new creation (1:18; cf. esp. 1:21). But faith must be exercised in sharing with the needy (2:15–16); otherwise it is dead (2:17). It can be demonstrated by works (2:18); otherwise it merely resembles the faith of demons (2:19). Scripture itself makes the point very clearly that "faith without works doesn't work" (2:20). From the fact that Abraham offered Isaac on the "altar," it is clear that "faith works together with works and faith is perfected by works" (2:21–22). The story of Rahab also makes the same point. James was concerned to reject a concept of naked intellectual faith, as would Paul have been had he come across such a problem. For Paul, faith is always shaped by the divine promise that calls forth the human action of trust. Although James does not actually define what he understands by "faith," he is clear that it must always be followed by the reflex of obedience.

CONCLUSION

We have seen several key aspects, then, of the New Testament's conception of faith. First, the content of faith is the identity of God and his action in Christ. In the three definitions of God we noted in Romans 4, each is prefaced by reference to believing in that God: "Believing in the one who justifies the ungodly" (4:5); "believing in the one who gives life to the dead and calls non-beings into being" (4:17); and "believing in the God who raised Jesus from the dead" (4:24). This content determines the structure of faith—faith is recognizing one's ungodliness, death and nonbeing, and trusting God to bring about the opposite in the future, just as he has demonstrated this supremely in the resurrection of Jesus. This faith, as Paul expounds it, is in radical contrast to the portrait of faith in Jewish exegesis. It is not to be fused with obedience to the law in the flesh, such as characterized the old age before Christ. Second, however, the contribution of James is that faith, although a gift, is not a kind of inert possession that can be regarded in itself. It must be exercised, and the content of faith must never be the sole aspect; it must give rise to action, as Paul also recognized. What God has joined together, let not man put asunder.

The Nature of Justifying Faith

BY DAVID VANDRUNEN

Thehe claim that justification comes *sola fide* was central to the debates of the Reformation. When the matter of *sola fide* is raised, however, attention tends to focus on the first of these words: alone. We remember that the Reformers taught that justification is by faith *alone* while Roman Catholics countered that justification is by faith *and* good works. Thus, it may seem, both sides affirmed the importance of faith, but disagreed simply on whether anything had to be added to faith in order to secure justification. This is true in a sense—both sides did speak of the necessity of faith—but it can also be misleading. It is potentially misleading because the Reformers and Roman Catholics disagreed about more than whether justification was by faith alone. They also had different understandings of the nature and definition of *faith*. In other words, the Reformation diverged from Rome not only in affirming that faith alone justifies, but also in defining the faith that justifies in the way that it did.

This dispute is much more than an historical curiosity. Christians today who continue to affirm that faith alone justifies surely must take care to speak about this faith accurately. If we are to make such lofty claims for faith, we ought to be sure to understand what it is. And disagreements about the character of justifying faith remain alive. Despite some development in Roman Catholic teaching on faith that may seem to bring it closer to the Reformation's understanding, fundamental differences still remain between them. In addition, in some contemporary controversies over the doctrine of justification in Protestant circles, certain writers have suggested an understanding of faith that also diverges from historic Reformation teaching. In this article, then, we will examine these different conceptions of faith and reflect upon the biblical teaching.

DIFFERENT DEFINITIONS OF FAITH

The Roman Catholic tradition tends to emphasize faith as an intellectual act, that is, as a way of knowing. Often Roman Catholic theology distinguishes faith from reason. Reason is taken as a way of knowing that depends not upon supernatural revelation but upon what the human mind can know by its own intrinsic powers. Through reason, a person can gain true knowledge of many things about this world and even about God. Some things cannot be known by reason, however, according to traditional Roman teaching. By faith, then, a person comes to know things not by virtue of the natural light of reason but by divine revelation. Such knowledge rests upon the authority of God alone as he speaks in the Scriptures and especially in the church. Faith informs people of some things that can also be known by reason, but also of many things that are beyond the competence of reason. Some recent Roman Catholic theology, under the direction of the Second Vatican Council, has attempted to broaden this understanding of faith as a mode of knowledge, but this intellectual emphasis still remains.

For Rome, then, this faith as a mode of knowledge was deemed necessary, but insufficient, for justification. To faith must be added charity, or love. Faith that is "informed" by charity justifies, while faith that lacks charity—a dead faith—cannot justify. This dead faith fails to justify not because there is something wrong with this faith in itself, but because the essential accompanying element of charity is absent. We will return momentarily to explore the significance of this fact.

In the light of this theological background, the Reformers felt it was necessary not merely to insist that faith alone justifies but also to offer a different definition of justifying faith that better captures biblical teaching. They did not deny that there was an intellectual aspect of true faith. Faith certainly involves knowledge. But they were also convinced that faith is something more than this and, in fact, that this something more stands at the heart of what faith is. Three Latin terms often used to describe this enriched conception of justifying faith are *notitia*, *assensus*, and *fiducia*. *Notitia* refers to an intellectual understanding about Christ and his gospel. *Assensus* refers to an intellectual assent to the truth of what is proclaimed in the gospel. But beyond these crucial intellectual acts is *fiducia*, an act not of the intellect but of the will, which may be described simply as trust. Much more than being a mode of knowledge, faith involves a sincere trust in Christ and his gospel for salvation.

Question and Answer 86 of the Westminster Shorter Catechism provides a concise and helpful statement of this insight. In response to the question of what faith in Jesus Christ is, the catechism answers: "Faith in Jesus Christ is a saving grace, whereby we receive and rest upon him alone for salvation, as he is offered to us in the gospel." Not only must the mind grasp the things about Christ and his gospel, but also the heart must rest upon him as the perfect Savior from sins. This character of justifying faith as trust in Christ has prompted some theologians to speak of faith as "extraspective." The term *introspective* is familiar to most people: it refers to looking within oneself. Something that is *extraspective*, then, concerns looking outside oneself. That is precisely what faith as trust does: it looks outside of oneself (thereby forsaking all self-confidence) and rests upon another, the Lord Jesus Christ, who has done all things necessary for our salvation.

In light of this enriched understanding of faith, some important differences between Rome and the Reformation become entirely understandable. Because Rome tended to understand faith as a mode of knowledge, it naturally juxtaposed faith with reason. For Rome, faith and reason are two ways of knowing. In contrast, Protestant theology has much more commonly juxtaposed faith with works. Because the heart of faith is not knowledge but extraspective trust, faith is most importantly to be distinguished from those good works that one might perform in order to merit salvation. From this perspective, faith is not a way of knowing to be distinguished from reason, but a means for attaining eternal life to be distinguished from good works. Whereas good works seek a self-achieved eternal life before God, faith forsakes all self-achievement and rests entirely upon Christ, who has achieved eternal life for us. This is why, for justification, faith must be *alone*. If justification required faith to be supplemented by any good works of our own, then faith would no longer be what it is—a forsaking of confidence in one's good works, and complete confidence in the work of Christ.

This also helps to explain the different understandings of what a dead faith is. For Rome, as previously noted, faith is dead when it is not formed by charity, but this does not necessarily mean that there is something wrong with the faith itself. For the Reformation understanding of faith, on the other hand, faith is dead when it merely knows but does not trust. This is an important difference. The Reformers recognized that dead faith entails a defect in faith itself. Dead faith is not simply faith that lacks love or some other accompanying virtue, but a "faith" that is itself not at all true faith. Without that extraspective trust that rests upon Christ alone, "faith" that merely knows facts is unable to justify.

Before we turn to reflect upon biblical teaching about the nature of faith, it may be helpful to note another view of faith that has become popular among some people recently and also differs from historic Protestant teaching. This view, which has circulated among some associated with the so-called New Perspective on Paul and the Federal Vision circles, seeks to understand faith as encompassing the broader idea of faithfulness. Faith, in this view, involves not merely trust in Christ but also the range of obedient good works that faithfulness entails. Whereas the Reformation insisted that good works must flow from faith as its fruit, while distinguishing them clearly, this other view sees both trust in Christ and covenant obedience as parts of a broader faith (or faithfulness) that justifies.

BIBLICAL TEACHING ON THE NATURE OF FAITH

The idea that faith entails extraspective trust in Christ can be seen in any number of biblical passages. It is important to remember that when Scripture refers to faith it does not always have exactly the same meaning of faith in mind. For instance, occasionally Scripture speaks of faith in terms of a general belief in the truth of God's Word (sometimes called *fides generalis*). Paul, for example, says in Acts 24:14: "I believe everything that agrees with the Law and that is written in the prophets." Also, the same New Testament Greek word that is translated "faith," *pistis*, can also mean "faithfulness." And thus we can find examples of Scripture using *pistis* in this way (e.g., Matt. 23:23). But what is critical to note is that in contexts in which Scripture teaches about salvation in general and justification in particular, it consistently uses the term "faith" to describe the extraspective trust in Christ described above. This is what theology refers to as a saving, justifying faith.

A first point that may strike readers as patently obvious is that Scripture emphasizes again and again that true faith is faith *in Christ*. But however obvious this may seem to Bible-reading Christians, it is not a truth that should be quickly passed over. It is not uncommon to hear unbelievers in times of anxiety or crisis saying things such as, "You gotta have faith." Yes, but faith in what? Biblical, justifying faith is not some general virtue by which someone retains a positive attitude in the face of uncertain circumstances, but a very specific trust in something. Or, much better, trust in *someone*. Justifying faith does indeed believe all things written in the law and the prophets, as Paul states of himself in Acts 24, but even more importantly it rests in Christ himself and the promises offered in his gospel. Whosoever "believes in him" will not perish but receive eternal life (John 3:16); everyone "who believes in him" receives forgiveness of sins (Acts 10:43); the righteousness of God comes "through faith in Jesus Christ" (Rom. 3:22).

This Christ-centered, gospel-centered faith is, in Scripture, a faith of trust, of confidence in the face of every earthly reason to doubt. Readers familiar with Paul know that Romans and Galatians are his two letters that deal most extensively with justification, and in both of these letters he looks back to Habakkuk 2:4 as a central statement of the doctrine of faith that he teaches: "The righteous will live by faith." The Hebrew word translated "faith" in Habakkuk 2:4 does not necessarily mean trust and, in fact, often means something different from this. But the context in which the prophet makes this statement indicates why Paul saw this verse as expressing his gospel so clearly. In contrast to their Chaldean enemies threatening to engulf them—who are proud (1:8), rude (1:10), puffed up (2:4), and who make their own might their god (1:11)—God's people are called to live by faith. Not self-sufficient and self-absorbed, they are to find their confidence outside of themselves—even when the figs, vines, olive trees, and fields fail to yield their produce, even when the flocks and herds are missing from the fold (3:17). Israel had no earthly reason to be confident, yet the Lord was their strength (3:19). Here is faith, an extraspective trust in the face of overwhelming earthly odds against them.

And so Paul finds Habakkuk's brief statement about faith a marvelous summary of his gospel in Romans and Galatians. We may note how Paul describes this faith that justifies, toward the end of Romans 4 in the midst of his larger discussion of justification by faith, and see how beautifully it corresponds to the sort of faith that Habakkuk commended many centuries before. In Romans 4:18–21, Paul writes concerning Abraham:

> In hope he believed against hope, that he should become the father of many nations, as he had been told, "So shall your offspring be." He did not weaken in faith when he considered his own body, which was as good as dead (since he was about a hundred years old), or when he considered the barrenness of Sarah's womb. No distrust made him waver concerning the promise of God, but he grew strong in his faith as he gave glory to God, fully convinced that God was able to do what he had promised.

Like the Israelites in Habakkuk's time, Abraham had no earthly reason to be confident about his future. He was almost one hundred years old and his wife was barren—their medical odds of conceiving were zero. But Abraham was not looking to his own efforts or to earthly odds, but to God and his promises. This is indeed faith constituted by extraspective trust. Abraham was not deterred by "distrust" (the opposite of faith), but was "fully convinced" that God would do what he promised. What he could not do himself, God would do for him. This is the faith that justifies, as Paul explains in the very next verse: "That is why his faith was counted to him as righteousness."

One matter important to note here is that faith, as extraspective trust, is different from every other righteous action that we perform. Unlike love, joy, patience, goodness, and all the other biblical virtues, faith looks outside of itself in order to rest upon and receive the work of another. Nothing else does this. That is why Scripture, and Paul especially, so emphatically and persistently draws such a sharp contrast between faith and works. Working (that is, fulfilling God's law and earning everlasting life by one's own accomplishments) and believing (that is, trusting in another to fulfill God's law and earn everlasting life on our behalf) are two distinctive ways that one might be justified by God. Earlier in Romans 4, Paul crisply spells out this contrast. "Now to the one who works," he writes in verse 4, "his wages are not counted as a gift but as his due." But, he continues in verse 5, "to the one who does not work but trusts him who justifies the ungodly, his faith is counted as righteousness." The very next verse speaks of God imputing righteousness apart from works, and Romans 5:16–19 explains that the righteousness that one receives by faith is a free gift consisting of Christ's righteousness and obedience. Thus, here again is faith: not working or obeying the law so as to earn a reward, but believing in another and receiving from him that obedience that could never be self-attained.

It may be striking to realize just how often Paul makes this explicit contrast between faith and works, or faith and the law—at least a dozen times even by a conservative estimate. In one of these passages, Galatians 3:11–12, Paul uses the very Habakkuk 2:4 passage considered above to make this contrast. He writes: "Now it is evident that no one is justified before God by the law, for 'The righteous shall live by faith.' But the law is not of faith, rather 'The one who does them shall live by them.'" That Paul distinguishes justifying faith from the demands of the law, from all of those things that a person would have to obey perfectly in order to earn justification oneself, is eminently clear here: the law is not of faith! Faith alone, Habakkuk's extraspective trust in the face of earthly adversity alone, not obedience to the law, is the means by which justification comes to sinners. Let one more familiar example from Paul suffice: "For by grace you have been saved through faith. And this is not your own doing; it is the gift of God, not a result of works, so that no one may boast" (Eph. 2:8–9).

Faith is trust. Faith is not one good work among others, but that which stands in sharp distinction from all good works in that it rests upon and receives the good works of another. Therefore, contrary to the claims of some contemporary writers, faith is not faithfulness. Faithfulness, and all other good works, will flow from faith as we are sanctified by the Holy Spirit. But for justification, God's declaration that we are righteous before him, one must make a choice: faith *or* works. Therefore only by faith *alone* will a sinner be justified.

BY FAITH, THEREFORE BY GRACE

One final point may help to put this discussion of the nature of faith in perspective. As we have considered the nature of faith as extraspective trust in Christ, perhaps it has struck you how amazingly appropriate faith is as the only means by which we are justified. Faith was not some arbitrary condition for justification that God decided to impose. It is not as though kindness or patience could have substituted just as well for faith had God decided to make one of these the only instrument of justification. No, God declared that justification of sinners would come by faith because faith is exactly the right choice for the job. Because it looks outside of itself and rests upon the work of another, faith is supremely compatible with a salvation that is gracious, that is, not self-achieved.

Paul makes precisely this point in Romans 4:16: "That is why it depends on faith, in order that the promise may rest on grace and be guaranteed to all his offspring—not only to the adherent of the law but also to the one who shares the faith of Abraham, who is the father of us all." Because this is a justification by faith, explains Paul, it is a promise that comes by grace. Is it conceivable that one could be justified by obedience to the law and still, somehow, preserve the gracious character of salvation? Paul denies this very thing: "You are severed from Christ, you who would be justified by the law; you have fallen away from grace" (Gal. 5:4).

CONCLUSION

From the Reformation to the present day, the battle for a biblical doctrine of justification has turned upon an understanding of *sola fide*. Justification comes by faith alone, but this is not just any faith. Justifying faith, unlike any other virtue, and in defiance of every earthly discouragement, turns away from itself, places its confidence in the victorious work of Jesus Christ, and receives his perfect righteousness as an imputed gift. By this faith and no other—by this faith and not love, faithfulness, or any other noble deed—the sinner stands justified before God. The gospel message continues to be: Forsake all confidence in yourself and trust wholly in Christ.

An American Tragedy: Jonathan Edwards on Justification

BY GEORGE HUNSINGER

I t is impossible to read Jonathan Edwards' long 1734/1738 treatise on justification by faith alone without realizing that one is in the presence of a very great mind. The treatise is as rigorous in argument and subtle in its distinctions as any of his other writings. At the same time, however, it seems fair to say that the virtues of Edwards' treatise are also in some sense its liabilities. One serious liability is the brief section where he tries to defend himself against the perception that his doctrine of justification implicates him in a doctrine of congruent merit.

Congruent merit is the idea that God bestows a reward not out of strict obligation but out of pure benevolence. Although none has been promised, a reward is nonetheless bestowed in proportion to the quality of the human virtue or performance that is pleasing in God's sight. Depending on the conception, the pleasing human excellence can be seen as at once grounded entirely in divine grace, and yet also as somehow relatively independent of the grace that makes it possible. The proportionality between the pleasing human excellence and the benevolent divine reward might be compared, in some sense, to a matching grant. The measure of excellence is somehow matched, proportionately if not necessarily equivalently, by the measure of reward. The reward is fitting though not obligatory.

EDWARDS' DOUBLE-GROUNDED DOCTRINE OF JUSTIFICATION

Edwards has to face the question of a "fitting" divine reward—"fitting" and "reward" are his own words—primarily because, in some sense, he makes justification rest on a double ground, the one primary, the other "secondary and derivative."[1] The primary ground, as Edwards states, is Christ alone; it results in the actual though virtual justification—again "virtual" is Edwards's word—that the believer enjoys "in Christ." A dependent and secondary ground is also posited at the same time, however, because faith is that condition "in us" that makes it fitting for us to be justified. Edwards is quite explicit. Faith, along with all it entails, is described as "that in us by which we are justified."[2] In short, justification finds its primary ground "in Christ," in his negative and positive righteousness, and its secondary or derivative ground "in us," that is, in faith, defined as a disposition, as a "habit and principle in the heart."[3]

Edwards wants to maintain two essential points at the same time. First, faith is that human excellence or virtue that, in some sense, makes it fitting for God to reward it with eternal life. Second, this idea of fitting reward avoids the pitfalls of congruent merit, because the virtue of faith is grounded entirely in the righteousness of Christ.

Faith is a virtue. It has, in some sense, its own "fitness and beauty." It is that in us "by which we are rendered approvable" to God.[4] It is that principle in us that makes it fitting for God to accept us, not because of any excellence it has in itself, but purely from the relation that it bears to Christ.[5] But by virtue of that relation, faith is "a very excellent qualification."[6] It is even "one chief part of the inherent holiness of a Christian"—Edwards does not hesitate, as we will see more fully, to use the term "inherent holiness"—that is pleasing to God.[7] Faith is a rewardable excellence only because it is grounded in Christ; but by virtue of being grounded in Christ, it is also, in a secondary and derivative sense, excellent and rewardable in itself. It is the thing in a person "on account of which God looks on it as meet that he should have Christ's merits belonging to him."[8]

"This is very wide from a merit of congruity," states Edwards, "or indeed any moral congruity at all."[9] If the idea of congruent merit could be restricted only to the case of independent moral effort, Edwards would be correct. His idea that it is fitting, relatively and indirectly, that God should reward the virtue of faith with eternal life would indeed have nothing to do with the idea of congruous merit, for faith is not a matter of independent moral effort. But the Reformation had insisted that our justification depended entirely on Christ, and not in any sense on some virtue in ourselves—not before faith, but also not after faith; not absolutely, but also not relatively or indirectly. Justification did not rest on any such virtue *qua* virtue in us, even if that virtue were faith. Faith was simply not a virtue in that sense.

Edwards knew about the Council of Trent, against whose view of justification he polemicized, but he apparently did not know about any more sophisticated forms of Thomism. He did not know of the proposal that virtues can be grounded entirely in grace and still be so pleasing to God that by sheer benevolence they merit the reward of eternal life, and that this reward need not necessarily be obligatory but only fitting or congruous. He did not know, apparently, that by defining faith as a meritorious virtue, regardless of how secondary and derivative, he had moved closer to Thomas than to the Reformation.

THE REFORMATION VIEW

Three basic tenets of the Reformation would seem to be contradicted by the aspects of Edwards' doctrine that we have examined.

First, as stated succinctly by Francis Turretin in his *Institutes of Elenctic Theology*, "What is inherent is opposed to what is imputed."[10] In other words, inherent righteousness is excluded by imputed righteousness from being, in any sense, a ground of justification or of acceptance to salvation by God. Following Calvin (*Comm.* 2 Cor. 5:21), Turretin observed that Christ's righteousness is imputed to us in the same sense as our sin was imputed to him: "Christ was made sin for us, not inherently or subjectively (because he knew no sin), but imputatively (because God imputed to him our sins and made the iniquities of us all to meet on him, Isa. 53:6). Therefore, we also are made righteousness, not by infusion, but by imputation."[11]

Since we are righteous in Christ alone, Turretin concluded (in opposition to the Catholic Bellarmine), Christ's righteousness as imputed to us excludes, as a ground of justification, our being righteous in ourselves. Imputed righteousness necessarily entails the corollaries that our righteousness (in any saving sense) is alien and passive. We never have any other righteousness in ourselves, with respect to salvation, than the righteousness imputed to us in Christ, and we never receive that righteousness in any other way than though faith. The righteousness that saves us is "alien" and not inherent, explained Turretin, "because if it is inherent it is no longer another's"; and it is "passive" because "what justifies as an instrument [i.e., faith] does not justify meritoriously."[12] While Edwards had a strong doctrine of imputation, he finally qualified it so as to admit inherent, active righteousness as a secondary and derivative ground of our being accepted by God, which if not directly "meritorious" was still "fittingly" patient of reward.

Second, as stressed particularly by Luther, "The whole procedure of justification is passive." Justification is not just passive at the outset.[13] As Paul Althaus explains: "This means that passive righteousness is not more and more replaced and limited by an active righteousness, and that alien righteousness is not more and more replaced by one's own."[14] Christians remain sinners throughout their whole lives. They cannot live and be pleasing to God except by Christ's righteousness alone, where "alone" is not to be qualified as meaning "primarily." "We live continually under the remission of sins," wrote Luther.[15] Christ's righteousness is not a ground that needs to be supplemented by a lesser and derivative ground within ourselves. It is rather the solely sufficient ground by which we receive mercy each day. Throughout our whole lives, stated Luther, "we are justified daily by the unmerited forgiveness of sins and by the justification of God's mercy."[16]

Finally, as emphasized powerfully by Calvin, we do not participate in Christ's righteousness without participating in fellowship with his person.[17] There are two points here. First, our union with Christ, according to Calvin, is a mystical union. It is a joining together of head and members, so that Christ dwells in us eternally and we in him. Second, and closely related, as Calvin affirmed, "The Lord Jesus never gives anyone the enjoyment of his benefits except by giving himself."[18] Christ does not give his benefits without giving himself, nor give himself without giving his benefits. Speaking of our union with Christ, Edwards confessed: "I don't know how to determine what sort this union is."[19] He finally resorted to describing it as a "legal union"—a union whereby one person is, because of a legal relationship, accepted for another, in the judgment of God.[20]

CONCLUSION

It is striking that in his treatise, Edwards often writes of "*something*" really in believers that justifies them at precisely those points where Calvin or Luther would more typically have spoken of "*someone*."[21] By casting *participatio Christi* in more nearly legal than personalist terms, Edwards finally ends up separating Christ's benefits, in some sense, from Christ himself. To be sure, Christ's righteousness is the source and ground of the believer's righteousness, but Christ himself as a person is not, as in Luther and Calvin, the exclusive object and content of that righteousness at the same time. If Edwards had seen union with Christ more nearly in terms of the mystery of personal communion or mutual indwelling, he might have concluded that the believer's righteousness in Christ was not just virtual but real, so that the believer's actual or inherent righteousness did not have to bear any weight in making the believer acceptable before God. Rather than the virtue or principle of faith, he might have seen Christ himself—the person in and with his righteousness, and the righteousness in and with his person—as that in us which (by imputation and exchange) makes it fitting for us to be accepted by God.

To sum up: Edwards clearly understood the intention of the standard Reformation doctrine of justification by faith. At the opening of his treatise he stated that "the act of justification has no regard to anything in the person justified, as godliness, or any goodness in him; but nextly or immediately before this act, God beholds him only as an ungodly or wicked creature; so that godliness in the person to be justified is not so antecedent to his justification as to be the ground of it."[22] As suggested by this very remark, however, he made a distinction between what obtained for a person before and after the event of justification, which coincided with the awakening of faith in the believer. Before the awakening of faith, the person had nothing in him—no suitable disposition—by which he could be justified before God. This situation changed, however, after the awakening of faith. Although Christ's righteousness as imputed to the believer was the only true ground of the believer's righteousness, it nonetheless entailed faith as the act of reception. Faith as a subjective act and disposition was then interpreted by Edwards as a secondary derivative reason why the believer was pleasing to God and rewarded by God. The idea of faith as a pleasing disposition that God would reward then opened the door to themes that the Reformation had excluded. Inherent as opposed to alien holiness, active as opposed to passive righteousness, and Christ's righteousness as a benefit decoupled from his person all entered into Edwards' doctrine in a way that, to some degree, undermined his basic Reformation intentions.

SHALL WE
STILL PROTEST?
THE DEBATE WITH ROME

CHAPTER 07

Not by Faith Alone: The Roman Catholic Doctrine of Justification

AN INTERVIEW WITH ROBERT SUNGENIS

*In March 2007, Michael Horton interviewed Dr. Robert Sungenis, president of
Catholic Apologetics International and author of several books on Roman Catholi-
cism, including the best-selling* Not By Faith Alone: A Biblical Study of the Catholic
Doctrine of Justification *(Queenship, 1997).*

CAN YOU GIVE US SOME BACKGROUND ON HOW YOU BECAME ROMAN CATHOLIC?

I was raised in the Roman Catholic Church even before Vatican II, as a matter
of fact, and so I know the Roman Catholic faith. At age nineteen, I decided to
leave the Catholic Church because I felt it was not teaching the Bible, that it was
steeped in ritual. For the next eighteen years I was a full-fledged card-carrying
Protestant. I was in and out of maybe three or four Protestant groups at that
time—Presbyterian, Baptist, independent, fundamentalist—so I got a pretty
good knowledge of Protestant theology. I'm a graduate of George Washington
University and Westminster Theological Seminary in Philadelphia, so I learned
from the best. Norman Shepherd created quite a stir at Westminster in 1980 to
1981 when I was a student there, and his emphasis was that works justify. I don't
think they ironed it out quite the way they wanted to back then, or even now, what
exactly he meant by that, so there was a lot of controversy. But it did stick in my
mind. When I was thirty seven, in 1993, I came back to the Catholic Church and
have been back ever since.

DO ROMAN CATHOLICS TEACH SALVATION BY WORKS? THAT'S OFTEN ONE OF
THE THINGS WE HEAR ON THE STREET, IN EVANGELICAL CIRCLES AT LEAST.

I would preface it by saying this: It's like the question, "Have you stopped beating
your wife?" If you answer yes, you're going to convict yourself; if you answer no,
you're going to convict yourself. So, it's a question you have to treat gingerly,
especially in a theological arena where things can be misunderstood easily. On
the one hand, I would say no, Catholic theology does not teach that one is justified by works if we understand by the word "works" that we are doing something
outside the grace of God. We cannot give God our works and say, "God, you owe me
salvation because of these works I have done." The Council of Trent condemned
that idea in its very first canon. It said that anybody who thinks that they can work
their way to God either by the law or any of their good works, whatever they are,
that's anathema. On the other hand, the Catholic church does teach that works
are salvific, that they *do* justify; but when they use "works" in that sense, they
are talking about works that are done under the auspices of God's grace—that
is, someone who has already entered into God's grace by faith, and God can now
look at those works a lot differently than when the person was *not* under God's
grace. When the person was *not* under God's grace, the law, which God would
use as a standard to judge those works, would condemn him for any work that
he did, because it would never meet up to the standards of God's righteousness.
But once he's in the "system of grace," as I call it in my book, then God looks at
him in a very different way, and thus those works he does for God, God can look

at those works, bless those works and give a reward for those works, which we call salvation. He in no way owes the man anything; he is not legally obligated to pay him anything for those works; God just does it out of his benevolence. And so in that sense, works do justify.

WHAT IS THE CLASSIC FORMULATION OF THE ROMAN CATHOLIC DOCTRINE OF JUSTIFICATION TODAY?

If you say "classic," then that would be from the Tridentine doctrine, and that was the last dogmatic council we had on justification. Vatican II and its aftermath do not claim to have any dogmatic statement on justification. All they do is reiterate what the Council of Trent said, and you can tell that by the footnotes in the Catechism when you read it.

COULD YOU SUMMARIZE THAT UNDERSTANDING OF JUSTIFICATION FOR US?

There are 32 canons in the Council of Trent. On the one hand, as I said, the first canon says that by no works of the law or any work done by man in his moral disposition can he attain justification. Justification is given by the grace of God. Faith is the beginning of the justification, and that's in chapter 8 of Trent. That is, that's the root of all justification. That's where it starts. In order to get into the grace of God, you have to have faith in God. Once you have the faith—and the Roman Catholic Church says that's a gift of the Holy Spirit as well—it's not something that you alone generate by yourself; it's you cooperating with God that allows you to have faith. That is, you have faith and works that are under God's grace, and both of those are looked at by God as things that he requires you to do, and he blesses those. As long as you remain in the faith and keep doing the works, then you remain in the justification. The Catholic Church also believes that if you do not do the works, that is, if you sin, then you can lose your justification. And you can regain your justification if you repent of your sin and come back into the grace of God.

WOULD THAT HOLD FOR INDIVIDUAL SINS? IF I COMMITTED A SIN AT ONE O'CLOCK, WOULD I BE UNJUSTIFIED UNTIL I HAD OPPORTUNITY TO CONFESS IT TO A PRIEST?

Depends on the seriousness of the sin. I like to use the example that Paul uses in Romans 4 where he talks about David. He says that David was a man who was justified by his faith without doing works; but if you look at the life of David, what we find is that David was a man of God long before he had committed the sin of adultery with Bathsheba and the murder of Uriah the Hittite. So if David is saying that he repented of his sin, and thereby was justified at that point in time, that means he had been justified prior to that and lost his justification, and now because he's repented of his sins (murder and adultery), he has regained his justification. So, in your example, the sin at one o'clock would be David's sins of adultery and murder, and then as he repents, he gets his justification restored to him.

WHAT IS THE STATE OF THE DEBATE THESE DAYS IN ROMAN CATHOLIC CIRCLES IN INTERPRETING JUSTIFICATION IN THE GREEK, *DIKAIOO/DIKAIOSIS*, AND THE LATIN, *IUSTIFICARE*? I'M THINKING HERE OF JOSEPH FITZMYER, WHO SAYS THAT CLEARLY THIS IS A LEGAL, FORENSIC TERM IN THE GREEK, AND THE LATIN, *IUSTIFICAR*, "TO MAKE RIGHTEOUS" IS ACTUALLY A MISUNDERSTANDING AND MISTRANSLATION OF THE GREEK "TO DECLARE RIGHTEOUS." WHERE IS THE DEBATE NOW IN BIBLICAL SCHOLARSHIP IN CATHOLIC CIRCLES?

We cover that in Appendix 2 of *Not By Faith Alone*, starting on page 615, where we deal with Fitzmyer's assertion. Basically, Fitzmyer doesn't speak for the Catholic Church, because there's been no official statement from the Catholic Church despite opinions from what we would call liberal theologians in the Catholic Church—and Fitzmyer would be one of them. Raymond Brown would be another, and there is a whole cadre of these individuals.

IS IT YOUR VIEW, THEN, THAT THE WORD ALWAYS MEANS "TO MAKE UPRIGHT" RATHER THAN "TO DECLARE UPRIGHT"?

Yes, we can prove that. We do it by a proof of, say, James 2, when James is quoting Genesis 15:6 where it says that Abraham believed and God justified him. He's quoting the same passage that St. Paul is quoting in Romans 4:3, so that means that James and Paul have to have the same understanding of the Greek word *dikaiosune*, because they're quoting from the same passage, Genesis 15:6. And here's where the Protestants try to change the meaning of *dikaiosune*—or *dikaioo* in James 2—because they say it means "demonstrated to be righteous" as opposed to "declaring to be righteous." So they have a dichotomy in their own thinking on the definitions of these words. We go through it meticulously in chapter 2 of the book to show that it is impossible to arrive at that position where you make a dichotomy between "demonstrated" righteousness and "declared" righteousness. We also show in the book that the preponderant use of *dikaioo* in the Greek is not a declared righteousness—and the same would be true for the Greek word *logizomai*, which is used in the King James Bible, for example, when it translates as "imputation." We show that the Greek word *logizomai* preponderantly means in the Greek that there is a *reality* to the thing that someone is viewing; it's not a fiction. It's not something that we label, not a label that we put on something, even though we know that the label is not saying that this thing is a reality of the label. We show that the Greek word *logizomai* actually means in the Greek that the label means what it is signifying. We go through all the uses of *logizomai* in the New Testament to show that.

SO *DIKAIOO* AND THAT WORD GROUP NEVER MEANS "TO DECLARE RIGHTEOUS"?

No, there's no passage we can point to that says definitively that the only meaning that can be applied here is "declared righteous." There's no passage we have found in the New Testament that teaches that.

SO IT'S ALWAYS A "MAKING" RIGHTEOUS?

Always, yes.

AS IN ROMANS 3:4, WHEN GOD IS SAID TO BE "JUSTIFIED" WHEN HE SPEAKS?

When we're talking about a soteriological context, then we're talking about that. We're not talking about passages that apply the word *dikaioo* to God himself.

SO THE WORD ITSELF THEN IS MORE ELASTIC THAN "TO MAKE RIGHTEOUS"?

Yes, but it's not elastic in its soteriological sense.

THAT WOULD BE A DOGMATIC CLAIM, THOUGH, NOT A LINGUISTIC CLAIM, RIGHT?

No, that would be both.

WHAT DO ROMAN CATHOLICS DO WITH A VERSE SUCH AS ROMANS 4:4–5, "NOW TO THE ONE WHO DOES NOT WORK, HIS WAGES ARE NOT COUNTED AS A GIFT BUT AS HIS DUE, AND TO THE ONE WHO DOES NOT WORK BUT TRUSTS HIM WHO JUSTIFIES THE UNGODLY, HIS FAITH IS COUNTED AS RIGHTEOUSNESS." WHAT WOULD BE THE TYPICAL RESPONSE TO THAT IN YOUR CIRCLES?

When Paul is talking about works in this context, he's talking about works that we do outside of the grace of God, and you can tell that by the word "debt" that he uses in Romans 4:4. He said if we try to work, then we're putting God in debt. And what he means is that it's like you're working at a job and you say, "God, I put in my forty hours, so even though I don't like you or care for you, I did work for you, so you owe me something." Paul says you can't come to God on that basis. You can't come to God saying, "You owe me. Here's my list of works; you have to pay me for what I did." Paul says in order to be saved, in order to be justified, you have to have a relationship with God. And faith is that relationship. Faith is the one thing that God can see within us where we know that we really want to know God for who he is, not for what he's going to give us. And that's why Paul is faulting the Jews here, because they got into a system where they were just working and said that God owed them salvation. God says, "I don't owe you anything. I want you to believe in me. I want you to believe in who I am." And that's why he uses the example of Abraham, because in verses 18–22 of that chapter he goes through what Abraham went through, an excruciating ordeal with God. God pulled every ounce of faith out of him because God wanted him to believe in God for who he was, and so, again, Catholicism really is not any different from what I think you believe here. Most Protestant commentators understand Paul's works here as trying to obligate God to pay them with salvation for the work that they do. Catholicism, as I said, in canon 1 of the Council of Trent condemned that idea as well.

BUT THERE IS THE EXPECTATION THAT GOD WILL REWARD OUR WORKS, RIGHT? THERE'S STILL THE IDEA OF MERIT IN CATHOLIC FAITH AND PRACTICE?

You have to be careful with the word "merit" here, because if we're talking about merit in a legal sense, we would say no, there is no merit in the legal sense. If we want to use it in the gracious sense, we would say yes, of course, and in that sense we merit something with God, same as Hebrews 6:10, which says, "God is not unjust when he looks at your works. He will faithfully reward you for your works." And it's interesting that Paul—and I think Paul wrote Hebrews, so I'll say Paul—is using the word "unjust" there. He is saying God is not unjust. He will reward you. So in that sense, there is merit, but it is a gracious merit.

I RECALL OUR INTERCHANGE ON THE QUESTION OF JUSTIFICATION AS A "LEGAL FICTION" FROM WITHIN A PROTESTANT FRAMEWORK. DO YOU STILL SEE JUSTIFICATION AS IT IS INTERPRETED BY REFORMATION THEOLOGY AS A "LEGAL FICTION"?

It depends on who you read on this topic. I've got a list of probably a dozen Protestant scholars in my book that I go through in chapter 5, dealing with this idea of forensic justification. What does it mean? I'm not really quite sure they do know what it means. On the one hand, you'll have a guy like R.C. Sproul saying, "Yeah, well, it's not a legal fiction because it's a real fiction"—even I get confused reading some of this stuff. They try to put a reality on the fiction. And somebody else will say, "No, no, it's not a reality. It is a legal fiction." So you get quite a variance on this topic here. This goes back to my treatment of the word *logizomai*. It's very important, this word, because a lot of Protestants are under the impression that this word only means something that you have a mental picture of in your mind but in reality does not exist outside your mind, and that's not the way the New Testament uses the word.

NOR THE WAY THE REFORMERS USED IT.

Are you saying you don't believe in legal fiction?

NO, IT'S NOT A LEGAL FICTION, BECAUSE THE RIGHTEOUSNESS THAT GOD DEMANDS IN THE LAW IS FULLY PRESENT IN JESUS CHRIST. HE HAS FULLY SATISFIED ALL OF THE CONDITIONS OF THE COVENANT OF LAW.

Where we would differ is this: We would go to Romans 4 again, and I would point out this same passage in Romans 4:18–25, "Abraham was fully persuaded that God was able to do this," and it says in verse 22, "*Therefore* he was justified, because of that." In other words, it's something *that* God saw in Abraham. He saw the faith in Abraham, and it's *that* reason that Abraham was justified. He wasn't justified based on some alien righteousness. It doesn't say that in the passage; it says that God justified Abraham based on Abraham's faith, and that's a real faith.

It's not a legal fiction. And that's the difference, I think, between the Catholic and the Protestant view.

BUT THEN FAITH IN ROMAN CATHOLIC UNDERSTANDING IS NOT JUSTIFYING UNTIL IT IS FORMED BY LOVE, SO WHAT YOU'RE SAYING IS THAT ACCEPTANCE OR JUSTIFICATION OF ABRAHAM WAS BASED ON WHAT GOD SAW IN HIM, NOT ONLY IN TERMS OF FAITH, BUT ALSO IN TERMS OF CHARITY AND GOOD WORKS?

Yes, you have to treat the whole ball of wax. When we're talking about baptism—and I think that's probably the better angle to cover this—the Council of Trent says that at baptism, hope, faith, and love are infused into the sinner, and at that point in time, he has all three of those virtues. So it's not by faith alone that he's justified; it's by hope, faith, and love at the moment of baptism. When you get to a case like Abraham, where you don't have baptism involved, you have to look at different phases of his life, and then you have to join them all together and make a conclusion as to what the Scripture is teaching in the soteriological sense.

HOW DO YOU COMFORT SOMEONE IN YOUR PARISH WHO SAYS, "I FEEL GOD'S DISPLEASURE. I KEEP COMMITTING THE SAME OLD SINS. I GO TO MASS REGULARLY, I CONFESS MY SINS, BUT I CONTINUE TO STRUGGLE WITH LUST, PRIDE, HATE, AND SLOTH." HOW DO YOU COMFORT SOMEONE LIKE THAT, OR IF NOT COMFORT, WHAT *DO* YOU SAY?

First of all, we would take him back to the theological basis for his complaint, and it's the same one that Paul had in Romans 7: "I love Jesus, but I find myself lusting." Saint Jerome said the same thing. He's there translating the Bible in his cave and he says, "I can't stop thinking of dancing women."

HOW ABOUT THE QUESTION OF ASSURANCE? HOW ABOUT IF SOMEONE CAME TO YOU AND SAID, "I AM CONFIDENT THAT I AM NOT ONLY NOW IN A STATE OF GRACE, BUT I AM GOD'S ELECT CHILD, I HAVE ALL OF MY SINS COMPLETELY FORGIVEN—PAST, PRESENT, AND FUTURE—AND THE RIGHTEOUSNESS OF CHRIST IS IMPUTED TO ME, THEREFORE I KNOW THAT I WILL BE SAVED HEREAFTER. I KNOW I AM ONE OF GOD'S ELECT AND I AM COMPLETELY FORGIVEN." WHAT WOULD YOU SAY TO THAT PERSON?

I would say you can be as sure as David was before he committed adultery and murder. David had to come to a point of repentance. He was a great man of God—he slew Goliath, he became the king, he passed up the seven brothers, he was a little shepherd boy out there, but Samuel chose him because God said, "I look into the heart of man, and he's the only one of all these brothers I'm pleased with." So if there's anyone who thought he was a man of God, it was David. And yet he sinned—terribly. And he had to be justified again. So that's what I would tell him. That's the example I would give him from Scripture.

SO AS LONG AS I AM MAKING USE OF, AS YOU CALLED IT, THE SYSTEM OF GRACE, I DON'T KNOW WHAT WILL BE TRUE OF ME TOMORROW NECESSARILY, BUT I CAN BE REASONABLY SURE THAT I AM RIGHT NOW IN A STATE OF GRACE.

If I walk out of the confessional and I've confessed my sins, and I go the next day and receive the Eucharist, well, there's no sin in my life that I can look at and say, "This is condemnable. I'm going to hell." Yes, I can say I'm a saved Christian. I'm born again and I'm on my way to heaven—that day.

HOW WOULD AN AVERAGE LAYPERSON KNOW THAT HE OR SHE HASN'T COMMITTED A DAMNABLE SIN? WHAT WOULD BE A NON-DAMNABLE SIN?

Again, there are two answers to that. One is to go back to David. David committed murder and adultery. Scripture itself teaches us that that was a sin whereby he lost his justification and needed to repent to gain his justification. So there's an indication right there. If there's any doubt as to what a mortal sin is—and that's what David did—it was a mortal sin, "mortal" being death. In other words, he was going to suffer the second death as it were for those sins, unless he repented. If there's any doubt about what a mortal sin is, then the person goes to the church and learns from the church, because the church is the one who has answers to these questions. He doesn't have to reinvent the wheel himself every day of his life and say, "Gee, I wonder if I committed a mortal sin here." The church teaches him because the church has been there, and that's why God gave us the church—to give us answers to those questions.

WHERE DID THE CHURCH GET THOSE ANSWERS?

From the apostles. And from the apostles, it was passed down through the Scripture and the Tradition, and it was transmitted through the Fathers until we have our knowledge today.

SO EATING MEAT ON FRIDAYS WAS A MORTAL SIN?

No more than eating meat that was offered to idols was in Acts 15, when the church said that the Christian should not do that. If anyone transgressed that law that the church laid down, they would be in sin, and they would be condemned for it. The same as Ananias and Sapphira were condemned for not giving money to the church when they said they were. They dropped dead and were judged right there on the spot. So these things the church *did* judge at that time, and it continues to do so.

DO YOU BELIEVE WITH TRENT THAT PROTESTANTS WHO DO BELIEVE IN JUSTIFICATION BY GRACE ALONE THROUGH FAITH ALONE BECAUSE OF CHRIST ALONE SHOULD BE CONSIDERED ANATHEMA?

The Council of Trent says—and you have to look at the verbiage it uses—"Anyone who says this, let him be anathema." But what the Council of Trent means by this is that someone who deliberately says that I know the truth but I am going to go against the truth because I believe what I want to believe, that person is anathema. So the Catholic Church has a lot of leeway for anybody outside the Catholic Church, because the Catholic Church knows through two thousand years of experience that people believe certain things because they've been taught that as a child, or because they're ignorant, or because of many other reasons. There are a lot of other contingencies why someone would believe something different from the Catholic Church. I think there is a lot of leeway as to who would be condemned and who would not be condemned.

What "Evangelicals and Catholics Together" Ignores: The Inseparable Link Between Imputation and the Gospel

BY R.C. SPROUL

H as the term "evangelical" become hopelessly diluted? All words, including those that serve as shorthand theological labels, are subject to the shifts of linguistic evolution. As every student of lexicography knows, word definitions are not only forged upon the anvil of etymology but are tempered in the crucible of contemporary usage. Thus, to determine what a word means one must look not only to the past but also, and especially, to the present.

"EVANGELICAL": PAST AND PRESENT

Etymologically, the word *evangelical* is derived from the New Testament word for "gospel," the "evangel" or "good news." In its most linguistic meaning, the term means (or once meant) in its adjectival sense, "gospeler." The chief historical significance of *evangelical* grew out of the Protestant Reformation as the term was used to distinguish Protestants from Roman Catholics. Since the magisterial Reformers saw the material issue of the Reformation as the dispute over the doctrine of justification, they were convinced that the conflict focused on the question of the meaning of the gospel itself. *Sola fide* was considered normative to biblical Christianity precisely because the Reformers believed that *sola fide* was essential to the gospel and, therefore, any "gospel" that either rejected it or failed to include it was "another gospel" and therefore not the biblical gospel. The chief protest of Protestantism was a protest about the gospel. The Reformers viewed the Roman Catholic doctrine of justification as a virtual repudiation of the biblical gospel. Initially the term *evangelical* was a term of antithesis, coined to differentiate sharply between Roman soteriology and Reformation soteriology. The antithesis was so stark that Luther could call *sola fide* the article upon which the church stands or falls, and Calvin could call it the hinge upon which everything turns.

In the centuries that followed the Reformation, Protestantism divided into multiple denominations and communions that differed from one another on a host of disputed points of doctrine. Yet this vast diversity of doctrine did not demolish an abiding unity based upon a common understanding of the gospel. For centuries, the twin affirmations of *sola scriptura* and *sola fide* served as the unity for Protestant diversity. This gave assurance that diverse Protestant groups, which subscribed to different confessions and creeds, could still regard their doctrinal differences as intramural debates among brothers and sisters in Christ, the people of God who share a common authority in the Bible and a common faith in the gospel. Historic evangelicals also shared a common "catholic" agreement regarding matters settled in the great ecumenical councils of the first millennium of Christianity such as the Trinity, the atonement of Christ, his resurrection, and so forth.

Again, for centuries the term *evangelical* served as a synonym for "Protestant." When Protestantism was invaded by nineteenth-century theological liberalism, which attacked not only the common understanding of the gospel and the normative authority of Scripture but also basic catholic tenets of historical Christianity, the term *evangelical* became used more and more to describe those within Protestant communions who rejected liberalism and clung to orthodox Christianity.

The modernist-fundamentalist controversy further sharpened the term *evangelical* to refer to those who still affirmed the historic creeds and who believed that personal redemption was an essential concern of the Christian faith. Evangelism was a top priority of evangelicals.

In recent years, the term *evangelical* has undergone more subtle changes. The most recent crisis for understanding its meaning has been provoked by people claiming the term for themselves while repudiating its historic meaning. The "reformist evangelicals" such as McMaster University theologian Clark Pinnock, et al., have distinguished themselves from "traditional evangelicals." While blatantly rejecting classic and catholic theism, Pinnock and others still claim to be evangelicals. At the same time, Roman Catholics have claimed the term for themselves while rejecting its historic usage. Keith Fournier calls himself an evangelical in the sense that he believes the gospel in terms of orthodox Roman Catholic theology. His appropriation of the word for orthodox Roman Catholics rejects the historic usage of the term as antithesis.

EVANGELICALS AND CATHOLICS TOGETHER, I AND II

In 1994, a group of professed evangelicals issued a joint statement together with Roman Catholic leaders entitled "Evangelicals and Catholics Together." Known widely as "ECT," the bulk of their joint declaration focused on the need for co-belligerence of Catholics and evangelicals working together to resist the influence of secularism in matters of abortion, political liberty, human rights, and the like. They called for a united stand against relativism in truth and ethics. But the document went beyond what Charles Colson called a "world-view" document to declare a unity of faith and mission between Catholics and evangelicals.

The publication of "ECT" sparked a serious controversy precisely as the point of the declaration of a unity of faith and mission. Historic evangelicals were distressed that such a unity of faith could be declared without a unity of the gospel itself, especially with respect to the doctrine of justification by faith alone. Pleas were made to the Protestant signatories to clarify this declaration. These pleas were responded to by the 1997 joint declaration entitled "The Gift of Salvation," popularly referred to as "ECT II."[1] In this document, points of agreement were articulated that the signatories believed set forth a unified agreement on *sola fide* itself, while issues such as the language of imputation, merit, indulgences, purgatory, and so forth, were left on the table for future discussion. Many professing evangelicals have lauded this new initiative as a remarkable achievement that at long last resolves the historical antithesis between Roman Catholics and evangelicals, so that the two groups can now see themselves as enjoying a unity of faith in the gospel.

Efforts in the past to reconcile the two sides have ended in an impasse over the grounds of our justification. Does justification rest solely in the righteousness of Christ imputed to us (*extra nos*: outside of us), or on the righteousness of Christ that to some degree inheres *in* us? The two views are manifestly antithetical views of the nature of the gospel.

The framers of the document insist that they are not speaking *for* their communions but *to* and *from* their respective communions. We note the importance of these prepositions: *for, to,* and *from.* What is not explicitly stated is a fourth crucial preposition: *about.* Sadly, the document proclaims a unity of faith in the gospel shared by both communions. They are saying something about two communions that obscures the historic antithesis.

As I have always considered myself an evangelical, I was distressed that other evangelicals were declaring to the world something about me that I knew is not true. I know that as an historic evangelical I do not share a unity of faith and mission or a unity of faith in the gospel with Rome. To be sure, there are members of the Roman Catholic Church who do believe the biblical gospel and as such are my brothers and sisters in Christ. But a blanket statement of unity in the gospel between Roman Catholics and evangelicals is irresponsible if what is meant by the term *evangelical* is its historic sense.

In the "ECT" affirmations, there is declared a threefold unity between Roman Catholics and evangelicals. This unity includes a unity of faith and mission and a "unity of the Gospel." Perhaps no aspect of this accord has provided more discussion than the declaration of a unity of the gospel. The controversy on this point recalls the heart of the Reformation debate, which gave definition to the historic meaning of the term *evangelical.*

"The Gift of Salvation" affirms that we are justified by the righteousness of Christ alone. This affirmation has caused many evangelicals to rejoice in that it seems to affirm the Reformation doctrine of *sola fide.* But before we analyze this, we must look at some preliminary considerations.

If the issue of justification boils down to two mutually exclusive options, a righteousness *in us* or a righteousness *apart from us,* how can the discussion be reconciled? We meet here a clear antithesis that seems impossible of being synthesized by some mutually agreeable compromise. To ameliorate the difficulty, I can think of three possible ways to resolve the dispute: 1) evangelicals could abandon their view of *sola fide* and its foundation upon imputation; 2) Roman Catholics could abandon their view of inherent righteousness; or 3) a formula could be drawn up that is a studied ambiguity by which agreement is reached in words but not in substance, leaving each side the opportunity to maintain its original position.

Which of these options, if any, was pursued by the signatories of "ECT I" and "ECT II"? On the surface it appears that it was number 3. That both "ECT I" and "ECT II" are ambiguous at critical points should be clear to anyone who carefully reads the document. However, the presence of ambiguity in such documents does not require that these ambiguities are *intentional*. To qualify for a "studied ambiguity," the ambiguity must be both *conscious and intentional*. We may wonder how it could be conscious without at the same time being intentional, but suffice it to say that both are necessary for a studied ambiguity to be "studied."

That "ECT I" has *conscious ambiguity* is without doubt. In a letter circulated to the signatories of "ECT I" written by Richard John Neuhaus, the chief Roman Catholic architect of the document, he asks the question, "Do we mean the same thing by the words used?" He answers his own question with the emphatic words: "Of course not." On at least three occasions the chief evangelical architect, Charles Colson, declared that "after all, we don't mean the same thing by what we said." In response to this disclaimer, I asked Mr. Colson, "If you knew you didn't mean the same thing by the words you used, how can you claim to the world that you have an agreement?"

With respect to "ECT II," one of the Protestant scholars who worked with the group declared his relief that there were "very few intentional ambiguities" in the document. Of course, if there were even a few intentional ambiguities that means, according to the laws of immediate inference, that there were at least some intentional ambiguities in the document. The question then becomes not if there are studied ambiguities but what they are.

It is at this point that *authorial intent* becomes of critical importance. It is also at this point that the letter of clarification offered jointly by Timothy George, Thomas C. Oden, and J. I. Packer, released by *Christianity Today*, is important.[2] Some of the explanations offered by these men are of crucial significance, since they were designed to answer questions concerning the "purpose and intended meanings of 'The Gift of Salvation.'"

The evangelical signatories stress that they do not claim a unity of faith with the Church of Rome but simply a unity with some Roman Catholics. They also explain that the accord is not a "complete common agreement on the doctrine of salvation as expressed in the official teaching of our respective communities," but is a "significant first step in the right direction." Further the writers declare, "We see our statement as expressing, not indeed unity in every aspect of the Gospel, but unity in its basic dimension."

I am pleased by the attempts of all those involved in the preparation of the clarification statement. I was personally engaged with some of these men who were involved in its writings. I am convinced that these men, both in their clarification statement and in their formulation of "The Gift of Salvation," intended to proclaim the historic evangelical position and are convinced that was basically accomplished in the accord. Some were effusive in their delight that their Roman Catholic "interlocutors" had yielded so much, including *sola fide* and forensic justification. They sincerely believe that they were able to achieve unity in the *basic dimension* of the gospel.

However, I do not agree that such unity was achieved: not only between evangelicals and the Roman church, but even between the evangelicals and the Roman Catholics who signed the document. I say this because I believe that the Reformation doctrine of imputation is a basic dimension of the gospel and that the Reformation doctrine of imputation was not affirmed by "The Gift of Salvation" document. What the letter of clarification states is vital to the question:

> The word *imputation* [not used in the body of the document] refers to God's crediting of righteousness to us because of what Christ has done for us: which means, God's accounting of Christ's righteousness to all those who are united with him through faith. As Evangelicals, we saw this teaching as implicit in the doctrine of justification by faith alone and tried to express it in Biblical terms.

I think it is clear by these statements that the evangelicals intended to affirm both the doctrine of justification by faith alone and its essential element, the imputation of the righteousness of Christ as the sole grounds of our justification.

The problem is, however, that "The Gift of Salvation" explicitly affirms neither *sola fide* nor imputation. Indeed the document itself, though it does not explicitly deny imputation, does implicitly deny it. How so?

What the document does explicitly affirm about *sola fide* is that some affirmations are "in agreement with what the Reformers meant by *sola fide*." That is, the document affirms things that agree with *sola fide* but does not explicitly affirm *sola fide* itself. It may well have been the intent of the evangelical signatories to affirm, unambiguously, the Reformation doctrine of *sola fide*, but the awkward wording of the assertion leaves that affirmation ambiguous. If it were unambiguous, we wonder how such Roman Catholic signatories as Keith Fournier or Richard John Neuhaus could have signed it while at the same time maintaining their allegiance to Roman Catholic orthodoxy and the Council of Trent.

The most problematic section of "The Gift of Salvation" is the section that refers to the urgent questions that are not yet resolved, which include, among other things, the language of imputation and the question of purgatory. The language of imputation is inseparably related to the concept of imputation. Without the concept of imputation, you do not have the biblical doctrine of justification by faith alone, and without *sola fide* you do not have the biblical gospel.

Michael Horton has used an analogy to illustrate the problem, using the metaphor of chocolate chip cookies. If one mixes together the necessary ingredients of sugar, flour, eggs, and butter but leaves out the chocolate chips, he may produce cookies, but not chocolate chip cookies. In a word, chocolate chips are an ingredient essential to chocolate chip cookies. Without the chocolate chips, one simply does not have chocolate chip cookies. Sugar, butter, flour, etc., all "agree" with chocolate chip cookies, but in themselves don't yield chocolate chip cookies.

Likewise, though we may affirm together important elements or "ingredients" of *sola fide* (such that saving faith involves more than intellectual assent and that justification issues in a changed life), without a clear affirmation of the imputation of the righteousness of Christ alone, achieved in his perfect active obedience (not limited to his work of atonement on the cross), *sola fide* is not affirmed.

To Charles Colson's credit, it was reported that during the discussions leading up to the final draft of "The Gift of Salvation," he steadfastly insisted that unless *sola fide* was included in the agreement he would not sign it. Colson is convinced that *sola fide* is affirmed and has declared that he could not see how imputation could have been made any clearer than it is in the document.

In the clarification letter, the evangelical signatories declared that the document was a "good faith effort" by some Roman Catholics and some evangelicals "to say with as much clarity as possible" how they understand God's gracious gift of salvation. No doubt the effort was in good faith, but that this effort yielded such clarity is doubtful. The signers of this letter acknowledge that the word "imputation" is "not used in the body of the document" but is "implicit" in it. Obviously, if clarity is the goal, the explicit is far more useful than an implication, which may or may not be drawn from the text. Since imputation goes to the heart of the historic controversy, we would have hoped that any attempt to resolve that controversy would have addressed it explicitly and without ambiguity.

Some of those who prepared "The Gift of Salvation" have complained that its critics have "moved the goal posts." That is, after "ECT I" the chief complaint was about *sola fide*; now after "ECT II" the chief complaint focuses on imputation. That this is seen as a moving of the goal posts only underscores the theological questions raised by this initiative. The goal posts have not been moved. The question of imputation is simply a question about *sola fide*. If indeed imputation is essential to *sola fide*, then it is incomprehensible how any evangelical would see them as separate issues that "move the goal posts."

Even more to the point is the question of purgatory. Purgatory and *sola fide* are utterly incompatible. As long as purgatory remains on the table, *sola fide* and the gospel remain on the table with it. If we are justified solely on the grounds of the imputed righteousness of Christ, that justification can be neither augmented nor diminished. I need no more purity to be declared righteous by God than the perfect purity of Christ, which requires no more purging of impurity in purgatory. As along as purgatory is affirmed, *sola fide* is not only implicitly but categorically, by necessary inference, denied. As long as purgatory remains on the table, there is no unity in "the basic dimension" of the gospel.

During the course of discussions of the preparation of the letter of clarification, I suggested that the statement read that the evangelicals were able to reach agreement on some aspects of the gospel but did not achieve unity in the gospel itself. It was granted to me by two of the signatories that they had not actually reached unity in the gospel with their Roman counterparts. Somewhere along the way, that reading was changed to its present form that declares a unity in the gospel's basic dimension.

What of forensic justification? The term "forensic justification" has been used in evangelical theology to refer to God's legal declaration, by which he declares the believer just in Christ by virtue of the imputation of Christ's righteousness to him. The letter of clarification says: "'The Gift of Salvation' affirms a declaratory, forensic justification on the sole ground of the righteousness of Christ alone, a standing before God not earned by any good works or merits on our own."[3]

Here is ambiguity with a vengeance. Rome has always had her version of "forensic" justification. That is, Rome recognizes that justification involves God's legal declaration that the believer is just. This is said to be via the righteousness of Christ. But it is the infused righteousness of Christ with which the believer cooperates and to which the believer assents in order to become inherently righteous. But, Rome teaches, God does not, and will not, declare the believer just until or unless that believer becomes inherently just; hence the need for purgatory. Roman Catholic theology emphatically repudiated Luther's *simul justus et peccator* (the reality that the Christian is simultaneously justified and yet still intrinsically sinful), calling it a legal fiction. Rome repudiates the Reformation concept of forensic justification.

Because "The Gift of Salvation" says that our standing before God is not earned by any good works or merits of our own, the evangelicals read this as a solid affirmation of *sola fide*. Yet an orthodox Roman Catholic could affirm the same words without meaning the same thing. Rome insists, as recently as the *Catholic Catechism* (1992), that because our good works and/or merits are wrought by virtue of the aid of the infused grace of Christ's righteousness, they are strictly speaking not "earned." This is the Roman version of *sola gratia*, which differs sharply from the Reformation view. (Neither Rome nor "The Gift of Salvation" document denies that believers have true good works or true merit, only that these do not "earn" salvation.)

To be sure, within the Roman Catholic communion there are crypto-evangelicals who truly believe the evangelical faith, just as there are crypto-Romanists within the evangelical communions. But this does not justify a public manifesto that declares a generic unity of faith and mission and a unity of the gospel between Roman Catholics and evangelicals. Such a manifesto at best confuses the faithful and at worst confuses the gospel. The "ECT" initiative is seriously, if not fatally, flawed since it proclaims too much way too soon.

Finally, it is sad to see in "The Gift of Salvation" that among those items that remain on the table for future discussion is the issue of the normativeness of *sola fide*. That leaves us with the assumption that even if a handful of Catholics and evangelicals did affirm *sola fide*, they do not yet regard this affirmation as normative to the unity of faith and unity in the gospel as such unity can be proclaimed without its resolution.

In conclusion, I see nothing in "The Gift of Salvation" that an orthodox Roman Catholic could not in good conscience sign. The document is flawed by its ambiguity at crucial points. These points must be addressed before there can be any significant resolution of the historic conflict.

Ten Propositions on Faith and Salvation

EDITED BY MICHAEL S. HORTON

I n an era when faith is redefined as a sort of religious power and salvation is merely self-help, it is more important than ever to be clear about what we believe about the cardinal doctrines of our faith. These ten propositions address some of the most contentious debates that are raging within American Christianity and that also form the core of the Reformation's complaint against Roman Catholicism.

1. It is impossible that saving faith can exist without a new nature and thereby new affections (love, a desire for holiness, and so on).

2. Saving faith is nevertheless not the same thing as such affections or desires, and does not include in its definition the effects of which the new birth is the cause.

3. It is not enough to say that we are justified and accepted by grace alone, for even Rome has agreed that it is only by God's grace we can become transformed in holiness. We must add that we are justified by grace through faith alone, and it is a great error to change the meaning of faith to include acts of obedience and repentance in an effort to make a disposition other than knowledge, assent, and trust a condition of justification.

4. The definition of saving faith is: knowledge, which we take to mean the intellectual grasp of the relevant historical and doctrinal facts concerning Christ's person and work and our misery; assent, or the volitional agreement of our hearts and minds that these facts are true; and trust, which is the assurance that these facts that are true are not only true generally, but true in my own case. In this way I abandon all hope for acceptance with God besides the holiness and righteousness of Christ.

5. Not only is the ground of our justification the person and work of Christ, the assurance, hope, and comfort that this salvation belongs to us must have Christ as its sufficient object and faith as its sufficient instrument.

6. While evidences of the new birth can be discerned by ourselves and others, such evidences do not have sufficient righteousness or holiness to form a ground of assurance or a clear conscience. For, as Calvin says, "A fine confidence of salvation is left to us, if by moral conjecture we judge that at the present moment we are in grace, but we know not what will become of us tomorrow!"

7. We affirm that, although no one will be justified by works, no one will be saved without them.

8. We affirm that it is contempt and presumption, not faith, that produce apathy with regard to the commands of God.

9. He seeks to tear Christ apart who imagines a Savior without a Lord. Christ offers no priesthood outside his prophetic ministry and kingly reign.

10. Those who are confident that because they have exercised their will or mind in such a way, God is obligated thereby to save them, show contempt for God's holiness and Christ's cross.

The Doctrine
of Justification:
The Article on
which the Church
Stands or Falls

BY J.A.O. PREUS III

"hat's the big deal?" Why are we harping so much on the doctrine of justification? What's at stake and why are we so nitpicky about it? Well, good question. Of course, we are not the first to "harp" on this doctrine. We think of ourselves as following in the footsteps of Luther and Calvin and the other great Reformers of the sixteenth century in focusing on what counts most. That's why we talk so much about Reformation theology. According to the Reformers, the gospel of God's free grace for sinners on account of Christ is central to our faith. We're simply trying once again to restore that to the preeminent place, where it belongs.

We also criticize the state of contemporary evangelicalism. The reason for our concern is that we're convinced the Reformers were right when they put the gospel at the center of their theological thinking. This understanding should be clear especially among people who call themselves evangelicals. The Greek word for "gospel" is *euangelion*, from which we get our English word *evangelical*. Properly speaking, to be evangelical means to be gospel centered. Yet, much of contemporary evangelicalism has been untrue to its name by supplanting the gospel-centered character of Reformation theology with a man-centered focus, such as our response of love or our obedience or the like. This is what has caused us to be so vociferous in our harping. Let's take a look at some of the rich truths of the Reformed faith.

THE GOSPEL AND THE DOCTRINE OF JUSTIFICATION

The classical Reformed and Lutheran traditions have maintained that the doctrine of justification is the *articulus stantis et cadentis ecclesiae*, the article upon which the church stands and falls. What we're really saying is that the gospel—that is, the good news that God justifies sinners by grace, through faith on account of Christ—is the *articulus stantis et cadentis ecclesiae*. So, in the minds of the Reformers, the doctrine of justification is synonymous with the gospel. When they spoke that way they intended to affirm the absolute necessity, for the church's continuing existence, of the message of the gospel. The message that sinners are justified before God by grace, for Christ's sake, through faith alone, apart from works of the law is absolutely necessary for the church to be the church.

According to the Reformers, this gospel (or the doctrine of justification) stands over the church as the criterion of the church's authenticity. It is the judge of what is truly the church and what is not. It is the presence of this gospel, in its verbal or visible forms (i.e., Word and Sacraments) that identifies the church of Jesus Christ and distinguishes it from every other organization or sect. Where this gospel is, there you have the church. Where you do not have evidence of this gospel, you do not have visible and therefore trustworthy evidence of the church. It is true that only God can see into the heart to determine if a person has faith. God can discern the true church in its inner (or invisible) sense. But we cannot see into the heart. We are limited to what we can see. We can see and hear the gospel. So the gospel, or the doctrine of justification, becomes the only visible or audible indicator of the existence of the church.

However, the gospel not only serves as an infallible mark of the church, it also stands under the church as its only firm foundation. Luther said that without this gospel the church cannot stand, not even for one hour. It is the substance of the faith, the substratum, and the foundation upon which theology, the church, and faith stand. So it not only tells us where the church is, but it is also the very substance of the faith, which nourishes and sustains faith and keeps the church in existence.

The Reformation leaders of the sixteenth and seventeenth centuries used to speak of this doctrine as the "cardinal article" of the Christian faith. This comes from the Latin word *cardo*, which means "hinge." The idea here is that the doctrine of justification is like the linchpin upon which the entirety of Christian doctrine hangs, or around which it revolves. This word was used to speak of the earth's axis, or as a chief fact upon which other facts depend. Without the hinge, the door falls. It loses its proper axis. Without the foundation, the church simply falls apart. It's very simple: Without the doctrine of justification you lose everything.

So where do we find out about this chief doctrine? The Reformers insisted that the only proper source and norm for theology was Holy Scripture. In fact, they were so adamant that only the Bible be used as the source material for theology and practice, they used the phrase *sola scriptura* ("Scripture alone"). Our cardinal article of faith is not something we choose. Instead, the Bible tells us what it is. The Reformers believed that the purpose of Scripture was to tell us of God's gracious and miraculous provision for the salvation of lost and sinful humanity in the person and work of Jesus Christ. His suffering, death, and resurrection form the heart of the scriptural teaching. Jesus himself affirmed this when he said, "You diligently study the Scriptures because you think that by them you possess eternal life. These are the Scriptures that testify about me" (John 5:39).

THE JUSTIFICATION OF SINNERS: THE DIVINE SOLUTION TO THE HUMAN PROBLEM

Now that we've seen that the doctrine of justification is crucial, let's take a closer look at it to see its essential components. The apostle Paul does a very helpful job of identifying these elements in his masterful summary of the doctrine of justification in Romans 3:21–24: "But now a righteousness [or justification] from God, apart from law, has been made known, to which the Law and the Prophets testify. This righteousness [or justification] from God comes through faith in Jesus Christ to all who believe. There is no difference, for all have sinned and fall short of the glory of God, and are justified freely by his grace through the redemption that came by Christ Jesus." In the passage, Paul identifies four integral parts to the doctrine of justification. One is justified before God: 1) apart from law; 2) freely by his grace; 3) through the redemption that came by Christ Jesus; and 4) through faith. Here then is a good working definition of the doctrine of justification (or the gospel) according to Romans 3: We are justified (or saved) apart from our own merits, by grace, on account of Christ, through faith.

As we seek a clearer definition of the gospel, it may be helpful to clarify what this gospel stands against. In other words, we can discern its meaning by coming to grips with what it opposes. If the gospel can be viewed as the solution to the problem of the law, then we must understand the law ultimately as a concern *coram Deo*, that is, before God (see Rom. 3:19–20). The gospel is only the good news that Scripture says it is if it comes as the solution to the problem of God, his wrath, his condemnation, his estrangement from us because of our sin. In a sense, the real human predicament is the God who judges; the God in the light of whose law we stand accused, or in the light of whose life we are dead, or in the light of whose perfection we are defiled. There are many ways to say it, but no matter what language one uses, we end in the same place: on the wrong end of God's righteous anger (Eph. 2:3).

To be sure, the effects of the law are also a problem among people. Sin is a social, anthropological, psychological, and perhaps even genetic problem. But sin is not first or even primarily this—as sinful humans, our real problem is God. We need a solution to the problem of God, to the problem that has a name, the problem who is God. It may sound strange, even blasphemous to say it that way, but our real problem as sinners is not merely that our sins are harmful to us or to our neighbors. Our real problem is that God is angry and personally offended by our sins. God's anger and wrath need appeasement. Our real problem has a name, and his name is God (see Rom. 5:10, in which we are spoken of as God's enemies).

The gospel, or the doctrine of justification, describes the solution to just such a problem. This means that the gospel is, in the first instance, a theological category: It describes how it is with us before God. It tells the good news of what God has done for us in Christ to solve the problem of him. This is a point made abundantly clear by Paul in his extraordinary presentation of the gospel in Romans 3. He says, "There is no fear of God" (v. 18), "the whole world [is] held accountable to God" (v. 19), "no one will be declared righteous in his sight by observing the law" (v. 20), "but now a righteousness from God...has been made known" (v. 21), and so forth. The most important result of Christ's perfect obedience is that God's wrath was turned away and that he turned a favorable gaze upon us (2 Cor. 5:19).

Thus, the gospel first of all finds its center in the work of God in Christ. This is its primary defining component of meaning. The doctrine of justification tells what God has done in the historical events associated with the earthly ministry of Jesus Christ in first-century Palestine. It is therefore as the Reformation theologians said, *extra nos*—that is, outside of us. Its focus and center is in Christ.

Secondly, it refers to the work God did for us (*pro nobis*), in the historical actions of Christ on the cross. Although we rejoice in what God is doing in those whom he justifies, that is more properly referred to as the fruit or result of the gospel (that is, sanctification), rather than the gospel itself. The doctrine of justification, of course, brings about abundant fruit (Gal. 5:22). And that is very important for Christians, since we have been saved for a life of service to God and to one another (Eph. 2:10). However, the gospel is about what God did for us in Christ, not what God does in us or through us as a result of what Christ did.

Third, since it is genuinely "gospel" (i.e., good news), the doctrine of justification stresses the sole sufficiency of Christ's work on behalf of the world on Good Friday and Easter (*solo Christo*). It is a word of God located specifically and narrowly in Christ's obedience (active in his living and passive in his dying). This good word was consummated at the cross and announced victoriously at the resurrection of our Lord. Seated at the right hand of the Father in glory, the risen Lord awaits the last day when he will return to judge the living and the dead.

Thus, in the fourth place, the doctrine of justification recognizes and genuinely honors the fact that our favorable standing before God is due solely to the grace of God *(sola gratia)*. Placing the gospel at the center, therefore, means that we will give credit for our salvation nowhere except to God in Christ. The credit is laid nowhere else: not to God's transforming work in us, nor to our faith or good works or love or obedience. The gospel gives the glory to God alone (*soli Deo gloria*), for God's grace is the sole sufficient cause of our salvation before God.

Finally, speaking of the gospel in a way that places Christ at the center means we must acknowledge that a person's salvation is brought about alone through faith (*sola fide*, see Rom. 1:17), as a means of receiving the benefits of Christ's work on the cross. This means that one can only very carefully speak of faith as a "cause" of salvation. We are not saved because of our faith. We are redeemed through faith as a means of receiving the already perfect redemption worked out by Christ on the cross. Only in this way does Christ receive all the glory for our salvation (Rom. 11:36).

CONCLUSION

We have seen that the doctrine of justification by grace on account of Christ through faith is an essential. It is the hinge upon which it all hangs, and the foundation upon which it all stands. The reason it's so important is that bound up with it are such central Christian and biblical truths as Scripture alone, grace alone, Christ alone, and faith alone.

Reformation Christians should be committed to these truths and to their proclamation in our world today. We believe that much of contemporary American evangelicalism has lost its center in the gospel. The doctrine of justification is, to put it simply, central. Nothing in us, not even the work of God in us through faith, can take the place of what Jesus did for us on the cross in history. Our sole purpose is to restore this beautiful doctrine, and the *solas* that form its heart, to the central place given to it by Scripture and the Reformers. Only this precious teaching gives full glory to Christ and maximum comfort to troubled consciences.

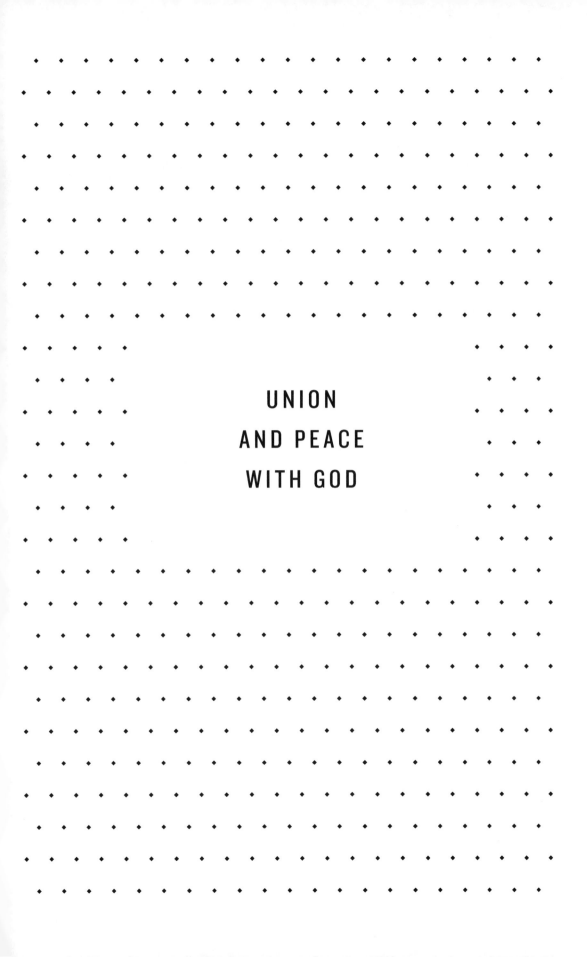

UNION
AND PEACE
WITH GOD

A More Perfect Union? Justification and Union with Christ

BY JOHN V. FESKO

Marriage is the union between a man and a woman where the two individuals become one flesh, as the apostle Paul tells us in the fifth chapter of Ephesians. The marital union, however, is a relationship that points to the greater relationship between Christ and the church. Typically, Reformed theologians have described the relationship between Christ and the church in terms of the believer's *mystical union* with Christ. Louis Berkhof gives us a typical definition of union with Christ: "That intimate, vital, and spiritual union between Christ and his people, in virtue of which he is the source of their life and strength, of their blessedness and salvation."[1] Union with Christ is also called *mystical* because, as A. A. Hodge explains, "it so far transcends all the analogies of earthly relationships, in the intimacy of its communion, in the transforming power of its influence, and in the excellence of its consequences."[2] While there is an exception to every rule, the doctrine of the believer's union with Christ is universally accepted in the Reformed community. Where disagreement lies, however, is the nature of the relationship between the doctrines of union with Christ and justification by faith alone. What is the doctrine of justification? We find a good concise definition in the Westminster Shorter Catechism: "Justification is an act of God's free grace, wherein he pardons all our sins, and accepts us as righteous in his sight, only for the righteousness of Christ imputed to us, and received by faith alone" (Q/A 33).

Dispensing with the inerrancy and unity of the Bible's teaching, nineteenth-century Protestant liberalism was fond of not only pitting Jesus against Paul but also pitting Paul against himself.[3] There was a legal-forensic Paul who gave us the doctrine of justification and the mystical-relational Paul who emphasized union with Christ. At the end of the day, the "relational" Paul won out. Now, such conclusions are only natural for one with liberal assumptions about the Bible. However, it might surprise some that we can find similar patterns in conservative Reformed circles. We will first survey some of the recent claims concerning the supposed incompatibility of the so-called legal and relational, or justification and union with Christ. Then we will offer a positive formulation of the proper relationship between the two doctrines.

DISHARMONY BETWEEN JUSTIFICATION AND UNION WITH CHRIST

Bishop and Pauline scholar N. T. Wright is well known for his rejection of the doctrine of the imputed righteousness of Christ. He argues that everything one would receive through imputation, one receives through union with Christ. Union with Christ makes imputation a redundancy. While Wright does not specifically state it in these terms, his rejection of imputation seems to rely upon the older tendency pointed out above, to subsume the order of salvation (*ordo salutis*) to union with Christ. For example, Wright argues that the

Reformed understanding of the order of salvation, while perhaps reflective of the Reformed tradition, is not necessarily reflective of Paul's theology.[4]

Rich Lusk, a former Presbyterian Church in America (PCA) and current Confederation of Reformed Evangelical Churches (CREC) pastor, has a similar understanding of the relationship between justification and union with Christ. Lusk also sees a conflicting tension between the legal and relational categories in traditional Reformed theology: "The covenant of works construction strikes at the filial nature of covenant sonship. Adam was God's son, not his employee."[5] Given the supposed incompatibility of the legal and relational, it should be no surprise that Lusk allows the believer's union with Christ to swallow legal aspects of the believer's justification:

> This justification requires no transfer or imputation of anything. It does not force us to reify "righteousness" into something that can be shuffled around in heavenly accounting books. Rather because I am in the Righteous One and the Vindicated One, I am righteous and vindicated. My in-Christ-ness makes imputation redundant. I do not need the moral content of his life of righteousness transferred to me; what I need is a share in the forensic verdict passed over him at the resurrection. Union with Christ is therefore key.[6]

Here Lusk argues that union with Christ makes legal elements of the believer's justification redundant and unnecessary, specifically that of the imputed active obedience of Christ.

Recall that in the historic Reformed understanding of justification, the believer receives the forgiveness of sins on account of Christ's suffering not only on the cross but throughout his life, which theologians have called his passive obedience. The term *passive obedience* comes from the Latin word *passio*, which means suffering. At the same time, the believer also receives the imputation, the accrediting, of Christ's *active obedience*, Christ's fulfillment of the law on behalf of the believer. Christ's active obedience is also called his *righteousness*; hence theologians will talk of the imputation of Christ's righteousness or his active obedience. It is this legal element of justification that Lusk argues is redundant and unnecessary. These conclusions seem to be based upon his understanding that a believer is a son, a relational concept, and that our redemption is more comprehensively understood in terms of our union with Christ rather than the doctrine of imputation, a supposed legal category. In this regard, it appears as though Lusk has tried to suggest a better way to understand the doctrine of justification, and in so doing offers what he and others believe is a more perfect understanding of our union with Christ.

There are multiple problems with such an understanding of the relationship between the doctrines of justification and union with Christ. We can address these problems and, more positively, set forth the historic Reformed understanding of the relationship between justification and union with Christ.

POSITIVE FORMULATION: THE BIBLICAL DATA

We find a host of New Testament references primarily in Paul's letters that refer to the believer being "in Christ." There are some twenty-five occurrences of this phrase in Paul's Epistles alone. One of the most explicit passages of Scripture of the doctrine of union with Christ is in Ephesians 5. Paul writes that the husband and the wife—when viewed through the lens of marriage—are one single entity, one body, and he likens marriage to Christ's relationship to the church. There are other images in the Scriptures that relate to the believer's union with Christ: the vine and the branches (John 15:5), the foundation of the temple (1 Pet. 2:4–5), and as head and body (Eph. 4:4–6). Looking at some of the other biblical data, we also find that union with Christ undergirds multiple aspects of our redemption, such as our predestination (Eph. 1:4), justification (Rom. 8:1), sanctification (1 Cor. 1:30), and glorification (1 Cor. 15:22). How do we interpret and relate these references?

UNION WITH CHRIST AND THE ORDER OF SALVATION

Historically, Reformed theologians have recognized that union with Christ is not merely one aspect of the order of salvation, but is the hub from which the spokes are drawn. One can find such conclusions in the theology of Reformed luminaries such as John Owen, Herman Witsius, and Thomas Boston, to name a few. That union undergirds the whole of the order of salvation is evident from Paul's bookend statements that we were chosen in Christ before the foundation of the world, and that only those who are *in Christ* will be raised from the dead and clothed in immortality. In fact, we may say that there are three phases of our union with Christ: the predestinarian "in Christ"; the redemptive-historical "in Christ," which is the union involved in the once-for-all accomplishment of salvation; and the applicatory "in Christ," which is the union in the actual possession or application of salvation. These three phases refer not to different unions but rather to different aspects of the same union.

Given these conclusions, it is no wonder that the Westminster Larger Catechism states that justification, adoption, sanctification, and whatever other benefits flow from Christ to the believer manifest the believer's union with him (Q/A 69). When we see that our being found "in Christ" underlies the whole order of salvation, including the legal portions such as justification and adoption, hopefully we begin to see how the Reformed understanding of the relationship between justification and union are not in any way at odds or redundant. From here, we can identify three concepts we must understand to have a proper understanding of the relationship between union with Christ and justification: the legal aspects of our redemption are relational; justification is the legal aspect of our union with Christ; and justification is the ground of our sanctification.

JUSTIFICATION AND UNION WITH CHRIST: THE LEGAL IS RELATIONAL

We should make two important observations concerning the relationship between justification and union with Christ. First, there is the unchecked assumption that because justification is legal in character it means it is not relational. For some unknown reason, the theology of nineteenth-century liberalism and contemporary expressions from Lusk, for example, both think that the so-called legal and relational are incompatible. Yet, we must understand that there are such things as legal relationships. Or, in terms of our redemption, there are legal aspects of our relationship with God. For example, Paul tells us that we have received "the Spirit of adoption as sons" (Rom. 8:15; cf. Gal. 4:5; Eph. 1:5). Here is a clear instance where we see the wedding of the so-called legal and relational categories; adoption is a legal term but also bound with it is the idea of sonship, a relational term. However, rather than seeing adoption as legal and sonship as relational, we should understand that the legal and filial are both relational.

One finds the same concepts inseparably bound in the person and work of Christ. Jesus was at the same time God's Son and born under the law (Gal. 4:4). Christ was obedient not to an abstract arbitrary law, but to the personal and relational will, the law in its legal demands, of his heavenly Father (Phil. 2:5–11). We must not uncritically adopt nineteenth-century liberalism's opposition between the legal and the relational. That opposition in itself rests on liberalism's rejection of original sin, divine wrath, and a propitiatory sacrifice of Christ. Not only are the legal and relational found together in the Bible, as we have seen, but even from common experience we know the two are compatible. Every day, people enter the covenant of marriage and do so recognizing that the legal bond is one that is also relational. A husband, for example, can fulfill the legal requirements of marriage and do so out of love. In the same way, Christ fulfilled the legal-relational aspects of our redemption in love for us, his bride.

JUSTIFICATION IS A LEGAL ASPECT OF OUR UNION

If we recognize the two points we have established thus far—namely, that union with Christ undergirds the whole order of salvation and that the legal aspects of our redemption are relational—then we must realize that justification is a legal aspect of our union with Christ. We say that justification is a legal aspect of our union because we should also note that there are legal overtones to adoption, as we have already observed. Nevertheless, if we recognize that justification is the legal aspect of our union with Christ, then to eliminate aspects of the doctrine of justification, such as the imputation of Christ's active obedience—something Wright and Lusk do—is to undercut the legal aspect of our union. It seems that both Wright and Lusk reject the imputation of Christ's active obedience as being unnecessary, superfluous. What lies behind such conclusions, however, is the idea that the Reformed tradition has invented out of whole cloth the doctrine of the imputed righteousness of Christ and created a redundant structure, one that can be discarded in favor of a more "biblical" construction. Such an opinion, however, fails to recognize that it is Paul who is able to hold together both the imputed righteousness of Christ and union with Christ without problem, hesitation, or embarrassment.

The Reformed tradition bases the doctrine of the imputed righteousness of Christ, even his active obedience, on such passages as Romans 5:12–21 (WCF 6.3, 11.1; cf. Heidelberg Catechism, Q/A 60). Why, for example, does Paul contrast the disobedience of Adam with the obedience of Christ? Paul writes, "For as by the one man's disobedience the many were made sinners, so by the one man's obedience the many will be made righteous" (Rom. 5:19). As John Murray explains, "The parallel to the imputation of Adam's sin is the imputation of Christ's righteousness. Or to use Paul's own terms, being 'constituted sinners' through the disobedience of Adam is parallel to being 'constituted righteous' through the obedience of Christ."[7] Clearly, Romans 5:19 restates what Paul has stated in the previous verse: "Therefore, as one trespass led to condemnation for all, so one act of righteousness leads to justification and life for all" (Rom. 5:18).

There is no mistaking the parallel between Christ's obedience, which is righteousness, and the imputation of this righteousness to the believer. Commenting on the abiding significance of Genesis 15:6 and the imputation of righteousness, Paul writes: "That is why his faith was 'counted to him as righteousness.' But the words 'it was counted to him' were not written for his sake alone, but for ours also. It will be counted to us who believe in him who raised from the dead Jesus our Lord" (Rom. 4:22–24). Note that here the English Standard Version translates the Greek word *logizomai* as "counted," which the King James Version translates as "imputed." Here Paul taps into the ancient stream of the special revelation of the Pentateuch, the first five books of the Bible, to argue for the imputed righteousness of Christ, and arguably also has other passages such as Isaiah 53 in mind when writing these things: "Out of the anguish of his soul he shall see and be satisfied; by his knowledge shall the righteous one, my servant, make many to be accounted righteous, and he shall bear their iniquities" (Isa. 53:11; cf. 2 Cor. 5:19–21).

We should also note, however, that in all of Paul's argumentation for his doctrine of justification and especially the imputed active obedience of Christ, he can write everything that we have surveyed, and at the same time also write without qualification or wincing: "There is therefore now no condemnation for those who are in Christ Jesus" (Rom. 8:1). If condemnation is the antonym for *justification*, then we can also reword Romans 8:1 to say, "There is therefore now justification for those who are *in Christ Jesus*" (emphasis added). In other words, a robust doctrine of justification that includes the imputed active and passive obedience of Christ is not antithetical to our union with Christ, nor is it superfluous. Rather, it is the legal aspect of our union with Christ. As Hodge explains, our union with Christ has a federal and representative character. Once again, what God has joined together, let man not separate.[8] This brings us to one last element to consider, namely that justification is the ground of our sanctification.

JUSTIFICATION IS THE GROUND OF OUR SANCTIFICATION

Why does Paul insist upon the imputed active obedience of Christ in our justification? Why is this necessary aside from the fact that the Scriptures teach its necessity? The answer lies in the nature of our justification. We must recognize that the ground of our justification is not our sanctification, nor the transformative aspect of our union with Christ. To base our justification in our sanctification is to change the judicial ground from the work of Christ to the work of the believer. The good works of the believer, even those that are the result of the sanctifying power of the Holy Spirit, are at the end of the day imperfect. In this regard, the Westminster Confession of Faith concisely explains why our good works, or more broadly our sanctification, cannot be the ground of our justification:

> We cannot, by our best works, merit pardon of sin, or eternal life, at the hand of God, by reason of the great disproportion that is between them and the glory to come, and the infinite distance that is between us and God, whom by them, we can neither profit nor satisfy for the debt of our former sins; but when we have done all we can, we have done but our duty, and are unprofitable servants; and because, as they are good, they proceed from His Spirit; and as they are wrought by us, they are defiled, and mixed with so much weakness and imperfection, that they cannot endure the severity of God's judgment. (WCF 16.5)

It is only the obedience of Christ, therefore, that can be the ground of our justification—not only the obedience he offered in his vicarious suffering throughout his entire earthly ministry, his passive obedience, but also his perfect law-keeping he offered on our behalf to his Father, his active obedience.

In terms of union with Christ and justification, Berkhof explains that "justification is always a declaration of God, not on the basis of an existing condition, but on that of a gracious imputation—a declaration which is not in harmony with the existing condition of the sinner. The judicial ground for all the special grace which we receive lies in the fact that the righteousness of Christ is freely imputed to us."[9] What we must realize, then, is that the ground of our redemption is the work of Christ; correlatively, we should also recognize that the ground of our sanctification is our justification. In other words, apart from the legal-forensic work of Christ, received by imputation through faith, there is no transformative work of the Holy Spirit. Or, using the title of John Murray's famous book, apart from redemption *accomplished*, there can be no redemption *applied* (see WCF 11.3; Larger Catechism, Q/A 70).

CONCLUSION

One cannot help but observe that much of the recent literature in the confessional Reformed community that pits imputation against union with Christ unwittingly repeats a false antithesis from nineteenth-century liberalism. While those within the confessional Reformed community undoubtedly hold to a strong commitment to the inspired nature of the Scriptures, this commitment is inconsistent with any assumption that there are *competing* models of redemption in Paul, the legal and the relational. In seeking to create a more perfect understanding of union with Christ, some have torn apart what God has joined together. If Paul's Epistles are inspired by the Holy Spirit, then it seems important that we follow the apostle in the construction of our own theology of justification as it relates to union with Christ. Namely, it is imperative that we hold together imputation and union with Christ, the legal-forensic and the transformative, all of which are relational. Let us not separate what God has joined together.

CHAPTER | 12

6-29.13

Justification and Sanctification Distinguished

BY KEN JONES

I t is a difficult and perhaps even dangerous task to take a single doctrine from the body of Christian theology and isolate it. You have to
ensure that the doctrine being extracted and examined is not given a
life independent of the body from which it was taken. In other words,
care must be given that the doctrine being singled out for examination
is not considered a part that is greater than the whole. The possible
danger of magnifying one doctrine is the risk of appearing to undervalue any
or all of the doctrines not being treated simultaneously. Having provided this
warning, scrutinizing the doctrine of justification by faith is a valuable enterprise
because it is so often misunderstood.

THE CORNERSTONE OF THE GOSPEL

Question 34 of the Westminster Shorter Catechism (Baptist Revision) asks,
"What is justification?" The answer: "Justification is an act of God's free grace,
wherein he pardons all our sins and accepts us as righteous in his sight, only for
the righteousness of Christ imputed to us, and received by faith alone." Of all of
the issues that fueled the Protestant Reformation, this one was most vigorously
debated and was considered by the Reformers to be the cornerstone of the gospel.
For Roman Catholics, justification was more than a legal or judicial declaration;
it consisted in God actually making the sinner righteous through the infusion
of righteousness rather than the imputation of the righteousness of Christ. The
concern behind Rome's position was that the Reformers were overthrowing the
doctrine of sanctification, thereby giving license to sin. Roman Catholics could
not fathom the idea that a sinner could be accepted by God while still a sinner.
This is the exact opposite of Luther's claim of *simul iustus et peccator* (at the
same time just and sinner). Both the Council of Trent and the New Catholic
Catechism (1992) state, "Justification is not only the remission of sins, but also
the sanctification and renewal of the interior man." In contrast, theologian Louis
Berkhof explains the Bible's teaching in his *Manual of Christian Doctrine* that
justification "is not an act or process of renewal, such as regeneration, conversion and sanctification, and does not affect the condition but the state of the
sinner." Renowned eighteenth-century Baptist theologian John Gill makes the
same point that justification is not "to be understood of making men righteous,
by infusing righteousness into them; for this is to confound justification and
sanctification together which are two distinct things....The word *justify* is never
used in a physical sense, for producing any real internal change in men; but in
a forensic sense, and stands opposed, not to a state of impurity and unholiness,
but to a state of condemnation."

DISTINCTION BETWEEN JUSTIFICATION AND SANCTIFICATION

For all traditional Protestants—Baptist, Reformed, and Lutheran—justification
and sanctification are two distinct doctrines and should be treated as such.
Berkhof defines sanctification as "that gracious and continuous operation of the

Holy Spirit by which he purifies the sinner from the pollution of sin, renews his holy nature in the image of God, and enables him to perform good works." It is not that Protestants overthrow or undervalue the doctrine of sanctification. To the contrary, we believe that the Bible presents justification and sanctification as distinct, and, therefore, they should be treated and defined separately.

The distinction between justification and sanctification is crucial both to a proper understanding of the Reformation's genius and, more importantly, for what it explains about the gracious character of salvation. For one thing, this distinction is what the Bible teaches. The fourth chapter of Romans is a thorough and clear articulation of the doctrine of justification. By this point in the Epistle, the apostle Paul has already established the need for the atonement: "There is none righteous" and "all have sinned and come short of the glory of God." He has also illuminated the dynamics of the atonement: "Being justified freely by his grace through the redemption that is in Christ Jesus, whom God set forth as a propitiation by his blood, through faith, to demonstrate his righteousness." This leads to the powerful statement of Romans 3:26: "That he might be just and the justifier of the one who has faith in Jesus." Having explained the dynamics of justification, Paul uses chapter 4 to illustrate this doctrine. Here it is worth noting that sanctification (or good works on the part of the person that is justified) is summarily dismissed as the ground for justification. In fact, a careless reading of this chapter could give the impression that Paul is not concerned about good works, but nothing could be further from the truth. The apostle's aim is to address the specific question of how a person gains a right standing before God. Sanctification is about our being conformed to Christ inwardly, but justification is about something different though related; it is about God's declaration of righteousness based on the imputation of the righteousness of Christ.

In Romans 4:2, Paul says that if Abraham were justified by works, he would have a reason to boast, and then in verse 4 that "to him who works the wages are not counted as grace but as debt" (this will be elaborated on below). The crux of Paul's argument is really in verse 5 where he states, "But to him who does not work but believes on him who justifies the ungodly his faith is accounted for righteousness." Again, Paul unequivocally divorces human works from the discussion of justification. So, this is not a distortion by Protestantism or the Reformed tradition. This is a biblical doctrine, and it is important that we likewise distinguish justification and sanctification as Scripture does. Failure to do so confuses these doctrines and betrays Scripture itself.

SAVING FAITH AS A GIFT OF GOD

Notice what happens if justification is not distinguished from sanctification. Saving faith becomes a work, because such faith would then include works or sentiments that somehow merit God's favor. This was true of the Roman Catholic system of penance and is equally true of many evangelical appeals and altar calls.

In both cases, sinners are called upon in essence to show sufficient cause for God to justify them. The Reformers understood saving faith to be a gift of God which, as Paul indicates in Ephesians 2:8, is passively received. Saving faith has been called the instrumental cause of justification, meaning that it is the instrument by which we receive or appropriate God's saving grace as set forth in the person and work of Jesus Christ. Many evangelicals, however, describe faith as a power that accomplishes something rather than receiving something.

Examples of this erroneous view of faith are certain ways of appealing to unbelievers to make a "commitment to Christ." While the intention is to press home the importance of being born again, a report on "Evangelism and Church Growth" by the Lutheran Church-Missouri Synod, 1987, makes an important qualification: "It is important...that the witness have a correct understanding of the nature of faith....Saving faith is essentially the reliance of the heart on the promises of ✱ grace set forth in the gospel. It is the hand of the alarmed sinner appropriating to oneself the forgiveness of sins won by Christ on the cross." In other words, exercising "saving faith" cannot be defined as "a commitment to obey and serve the Lord." The report goes on to explain, "While Lutherans believe that the commitment to dedicate one's life to the Savior will certainly follow faith, commitment is not a part of the essence of faith itself. It is instead a result or fruit of faith which belongs in the sphere of sanctification rather than justification." That is precisely the point. By defining faith as a human work rather than a divine gift, or by combining it with requisite affections such as penitence, we confuse the doctrines of justification and sanctification. This confusion leaves the sinner with the impression that God's grace is free once they have done their part which, as Romans 4 also points out, is not grace at all.

[handwritten margin note: RUNNING TO THE WRONG BASE IN T-BALL]

JUSTIFICATION AND HOLY LIVING

Confusing these two important doctrines also has important ramifications for the Christian life. It is almost inevitable that those who believe justification to consist of deeds or affections, which somehow unleash God's grace, will also have misconceptions about the dynamics of sanctification. In other words, if human works figure in the equation for justification, then the value of human works in sanctification will also be distorted. Contrary to what many evangelicals may teach or think, sanctification is not the basis upon which we are sustained in our salvation. If that were the case, then each time we sin we would be brought back to a state of condemnation. With such a mind-set, it would be difficult to maintain true assurance of one's salvation. There would be no way of determining whether or not one has done enough or has confessed every sin. Sanctification without a clear and proper understanding of justification produces a life of spiritual misery and uncertainty, or one of great self-deception, rife with notions of Christian perfectionism. Only with a proper understanding of justification can sinners recognize they are no longer condemned by God because (1) the righteousness of Christ is imputed to them, and (2) in his death on the cross, Christ has borne the divine wrath that was due the sinner. With this understanding, the good works of the justified person (which necessarily follow) are seen in the proper light, namely, as the genuine and grateful affections of a regenerated heart.

Justification and sanctification are to be *distinguished* but not separated. They are to be distinguished so that faith is not overthrown by works thereby nullifying grace. They are, however, not to be *separated* so that saving faith is not confused with a barren and presumptuous faith. As the Reformers claimed, "We are saved by faith alone but not by a faith that is alone." ✱

Properly distinguishing these two critical doctrines puts grace, faith, and works in their proper places, with the person and work of Christ at the center of them all. "But of him you are in Christ Jesus, who became for us wisdom from God, and righteousness and sanctification, and redemption, that as it is written 'He who glories, let him glory in the Lord'" (1 Cor. 1:30–31).

CHAPTER 13

Christ at the Center: The Legacy of the Reformed Tradition

BY DENNIS E. TAMBURELLO

hen I was preparing for ministry as a Catholic priest in the late 1970s, one of the professors in our theology program announced that he would be teaching a course in "Calvin's Sacramental Theology." At the time I remember thinking, "What could Calvin possibly have to say to Catholics about the Sacraments?" Needless to say, I didn't take the course. Years later, as luck would have it, I became a serious student of Calvin's thought. The more I learned about Calvin, the more I grew in appreciation of him, and the more embarrassed I was by the ignorance and arrogance of my earlier judgment. I came to realize that if I had been smart, I would have taken that course.

In this essay, I will reflect on the significance of the Reformed tradition for the Christian church, focusing mainly on the contributions of John Calvin. I speak as an outsider to the tradition, but also as an admirer. In our own day, thank God, we have been able to build bridges of understanding where there were once only walls of hatred and division. This is not to say that the walls have all come tumbling down. As recently as a few years ago, the Roman Catholic Church released a statement, *Dominus Iesus*, which in my view represented a major step backwards in ecumenical and interfaith relations.[1] This only makes it more important for a Catholic to engage in this kind of reflection.

I once had the opportunity to speak to a class at the London Bible College about what I liked and disliked about Calvin. It was interesting to discover that everything I had to say about Calvin corresponded to parallel things that I liked or disliked in Roman Catholicism. For example, I liked Calvin's emphasis on piety, which he defined as "that reverence joined with love of God which the knowledge of [God's] benefits induces."[2] This is the goal of knowledge of God—not to know God theoretically or intellectually but to give glory and praise to God, whom Calvin described as the "fountainhead and source of every good."[3] I saw Calvin's focus on piety as a point of contact with my own tradition's approach to spirituality. Indeed, in recent times, scholars have begun to speak without embarrassment of a spirituality in Calvin.[4]

On the negative side, I critiqued Calvin for being too sure of himself on a lot of issues—precisely a criticism I would also lay at the door of the Catholic Church at that time. In the sixteenth century, arrogance and pig-headedness were in ample supply, and Calvin's conviction about the absolute rightness of his own views was no more (or less!) obnoxious than that of his Roman opponents.

The exercise of compiling a list of likes and dislikes about Calvin was a helpful reminder of how much our traditions have in common even in their differences. With this in mind, I offer the following reflections on the contributions of the Reformed tradition to theology and to the life of the church.

THE GRACE OF CHRIST

Perhaps the most common thread that I see running through the teachings of the Reformed tradition, from Calvin's time to today, is the centrality of Christ. We see this in Calvin's own description of faith as engrafting us into Christ: "Christ, when he illumines us into faith by the power of his Spirit, at the same time so engrafts us into his body that we become partakers of every good."[5] One of the foundations for this christological accent in Reformed theology is surely Calvin's teaching on the twofold grace of Christ. This teaching is laid out with particular clarity in the *Institutes* 3.16.1, where Calvin argues that we have both justification and sanctification in Christ.

This articulation of the work of grace in human beings is one of the most significant contributions of Reformed theology to the church. It is debatable whether the Scriptures themselves posit such a clear distinction between the graces of justification and sanctification. Thus, Roman Catholic theology traditionally considered justification to *include* sanctification, i.e., the transformation of the believer. Calvin's formulation preserved the Roman emphasis on the importance of works, but placed them completely under the rubric of sanctification, thus avoiding any danger of slipping into the language of works-righteousness. The Council of Trent was not receptive to such a formulation. Today it is easier to see that Calvin's conception of the twofold grace was a healthy corrective to a theology (and more important, a piety) that had sometimes veered into Pelagianism.

Anna Case-Winters suggests yet another point that could be a "distinctive contribution" of the Reformed tradition: "For Calvin...sanctification is not primarily about good works, but about 'union with Christ.' We do not attain or even approach sinless perfection, but 'with a wonderful communion, day by day, he (Christ) grows more and more into one body with us, until he becomes completely one with us'" (*Institutes* 3.2.24).[6]

I would go further than this and point out that justification too is about union with Christ. Calvin explicitly makes this connection in his commentary on Galatians 2:20: "Christ lives in us in two ways. The one consists in His governing us by his Spirit and directing all our actions. The other is what He grants us by participation in His righteousness, that, since we can do nothing of ourselves, we are accepted in Him by God. The first relates to regeneration [sanctification], the second to the free acceptance of righteousness [justification]."[7]

SACRAMENTAL THEOLOGY

Another major contribution of Reformed theology has been Calvin's teaching on the Sacraments, especially the Eucharist. Contrary to what many Catholics have supposed, it is not true that Protestants in general deny the "real presence." In fact, in the Reformed-Roman Catholic joint statement on "The Presence of

Christ in Church and World," the dialogue commission stated: "We gratefully acknowledge that both traditions, Reformed and Roman Catholic, hold to the belief in the Real Presence of Christ in the Eucharist."[8]

Of course, there are some significant differences here. Calvin rejected the doctrine of transubstantiation, believing that it was a wrongheaded way of understanding the Eucharist. In his mind, it made no sense to speak of Christ becoming attached to the elements of bread and wine. Rather, he believed that in receiving the Eucharist the believer was drawn up into the life of Christ through the power of the Holy Spirit.[9] Calvin insisted that this communion was both spiritual and real.

Although I struggle with the teaching on transubstantiation, tied as it is to the archaic Aristotelian categories of substance and accident, as a Catholic I believe that in a real sense the bread and the wine do become "different" from what they were before the consecration. But Calvin was absolutely right in stressing that what was most important in the theology of the Eucharist was not what happens to the bread and wine, but what happens to *us* who receive the Eucharist in faith.

All too often in Catholicism, Eucharistic piety has centered on adoration of the sacred species. This focus misses the crucial point Calvin grasped: that we are the most important "tabernacles" where Christ dwells. The union with Christ we experience in the Eucharist should have a transformative effect in our lives. This was hardly a new idea in the sixteenth century. Several centuries before Calvin, John Chrysostom described Christians who came to receive at the Lord's Table, yet would not give food or show mercy to their brothers and sisters who were poor, as missing the point of the Eucharist.[10] Calvin himself followed Augustine in referring to the Eucharist as "the bond of love" that inspires compassion and care for one another.[11] Thus, Calvin can be seen as an important resource in current discussions of the Eucharist and social justice.

It seems to me that Calvin's rich theology of the Eucharist should have led historically to the Lord's Supper having a more prominent and more frequent place in Reformed worship. Calvin himself says in the *Institutes*: "[The Sacrament of the Lord's Supper] was not ordained to be received only once a year....Rather, it was ordained to be frequently used among all Christians in order that they might frequently return in memory to Christ's Passion, by such remembrance to sustain and strengthen their faith, and urge themselves to sing thanksgiving to God and to proclaim his goodness; finally, by it to nourish mutual love, and among themselves give witness to this love, and discern its bond in the unity of Christ's body."[12]

Calvin's argument here is directed against the teaching of the Fourth Lateran Council (1215), which required that Catholics receive Communion at least once a year. Note that Calvin is misrepresenting the council when he says that it decreed that Communion be received *only* once a year. This was the minimum, not the maximum requirement.

Be that as it may, Calvin's words can be turned against his own tradition, inasmuch as many Reformed churches celebrate the Lord's Supper somewhat infrequently. Calvin goes on to say in the *Institutes* that "the Lord's Table should have been spread *at least once a week* for the assembly of Christians, and the promises declared in it should feed us spiritually."[13]

This is one area where I frankly think Catholicism has been more on target with its practice, at least until recently. The tradition of celebrating the Eucharist on a weekly basis is an ancient one that the Catholic Church has consistently upheld as important. On this point, Calvin seems to be in agreement. Why, then, did the Lord's Supper come to be neglected in Reformed practice? Is it possible that the Sacrament was celebrated less frequently partly as an overreaction against the perceived shortcomings of the Catholic Mass? The good news is that there does seem to be some positive movement on this question in Reformed thinking. A good example would be the book by Keith A. Mathison, *Given for You: Reclaiming Calvin's Doctrine of the Lord's Supper* (P & R Press, 2002), which raises many of the issues touched on above.

Unfortunately, the Catholic Church is currently in no position to gloat over the priority it gives to the Eucharist. While proclaiming the Eucharist as the source and summit of the Christian life, our institutional leadership has allowed an intolerable situation to develop, whereby many Catholics are deprived of a weekly Eucharist because of narrow and outdated requirements for priestly ordination. Thus, in our own day, some Catholics end up having access to the Lord's Supper even less frequently than their Reformed sisters and brothers. Clearly, we Catholics have as much work to do in this area as the Reformed.

THE HOLY SPIRIT

Whenever Calvin talked about Christ, mention of the Holy Spirit was not far behind. This brings us to another contribution of Reformed theology: its pneumatology. Calvin's awareness of the role of the Holy Spirit pervaded every aspect of his thought. He defined faith, for example, as "a firm and certain knowledge of God's benevolence toward us, founded upon the truth of the freely given promise in Christ, both revealed to our minds and sealed upon our hearts through the Holy Spirit."[14] Similarly, he spoke of the Holy Spirit bringing us through faith to union with Christ,[15] and of the Holy Spirit as effecting the bond we experience with Christ in the Lord's Supper.[16] Following Calvin's lead, Schleiermacher theorized that "every regenerate person partakes of the Holy Spirit, so that there is no living fellowship with Christ without an indwelling of the Holy Spirit, and vice versa."[17]

This focus on the Spirit continues to pervade Reformed thought today. For example, in "The Presence of Christ in Church and World," Reformed and Catholic theologians proclaim: "It is through the Spirit that Christ is at work in creation and redemption. As the presence in the world of the risen Lord, the Spirit affirms and manifests the resurrection and effects the new creation. Christ who is Lord of all and active in creation points to God the Father who, in the Spirit, leads and guides history where there is no unplanned development."[18]

In our own day, much attention has been given to the Spirit's role in salvation and in the church. But historically, pneumatology has often taken a back seat to Christology. The Reformed tradition's emphasis on the Spirit has been a good corrective to this tendency. How much this emphasis has filtered into the everyday life of Reformed Christians is a question I am not qualified to answer.

RELIGION AS THANKFULNESS

I would not want to leave the impression that the Reformed tradition has only contributed to our understanding of God. It has also enriched the church's understanding of the Christian life in myriad ways. In closing, I would like to focus on a key element of piety that is rooted in the thought of John Calvin: the notion of thankfulness.

We have mentioned that Calvin defines God as the fountainhead of all goodness. For Calvin, the only proper response to God's gifts of creation and redemption is a life filled with gratitude, giving thanks and praise to God. Calvin expresses this point with particular poignancy in his famous "Reply to Sadoleto," where he argues that preoccupation with one's own salvation is theologically unsound: "It is not very sound theology to confine a man's thoughts so much to himself, and not to set before him as the prime motive of his existence zeal to show forth the glory of God....I therefore believe that there is no man imbued with true piety, who will not regard as in poor taste that long and detailed exhortation to a zeal for heavenly life, which occupies a man entirely concerned with himself, and does not, even by one expression, arouse him to sanctify the name of God."[19] This point is echoed in the *Institutes'* definition of piety as "that reverence joined with love of God which the knowledge of [God's] benefits induces."[20]

It is not hard to see how religion can degenerate into self-interest or fear. Even the most ardent believer in justification by grace through faith can fall into the trap of becoming preoccupied with his or her salvation. Calvin was accused of presumption for daring to assert that believers could have certitude of salvation; but he thought it obvious that if salvation is in fact God's gift, we should not worry about earning it. Rather, we should simply trust in God's promises and live our lives in thankful praise and love of God, expressing that gratitude in our love of neighbor.[21] This is perhaps the most practical contribution of the Reformed tradition to the everyday life of Christian believers.

The Discomfort
of the
Justified Life

BY JERRY BRIDGES

I am writing this reflection just after the conclusion of the high school basketball season. The girls' team from one of our city's high schools had a successful season, going all the way to the state championship game where they lost. The next morning the sports section of our daily newspaper showed a pathetic picture of some of the girls sitting on the bench watching the clock run down and knowing they had just lost the championship game. There they sat, chins in hand, looking quite dejected because they had been defeated.

We Americans don't like defeat, whether it's in a basketball game or in dealing with sin in our lives. I suspect that's why we don't like the seventh chapter of Romans. It sounds too much like defeat. It really isn't about defeat, however. It's about struggle—a struggle between the flesh and the Spirit. As Paul wrote in Galatians 5:17, "For the desires of the flesh are against the spirit, and the desires of the spirit are against the flesh. For these are opposed to each other to keep you from doing the things you want to do." This is a picture of struggle. Then Peter urged us in 1 Peter 2:11 "to abstain from the passions of the flesh, which wage war against your souls." Notice the war metaphor. There is indeed a guerilla warfare going on in the soul of every believer that causes us a great deal of discomfort. We don't like the struggle, and we especially do not like it when we feel defeated in the struggle.

Unbelievers don't have such a struggle. For the most part, they enjoy their sin or rationalize their sinful attitudes. They feel justified in their self-righteousness, their critical and unforgiving spirits, and their pursuits of pleasure and material-ism. Occasionally, they regret the consequences of their attitudes and actions, but they do not see them as sin. There is no guerilla warfare for the unbeliever. They may or may not have conflicts with other people, but there is little conflict within themselves.

Not so with the believer. The moment we trust in Christ as Savior, we are made new creations in Christ. The Holy Spirit comes to dwell within us to animate and empower this new life. He comes to deal with those sinful attitudes and actions, but they don't disappear overnight. They must be, to use Paul's words, "put to death" (Rom. 8:13, Col. 3:5). And that's when the guerilla warfare begins. The flesh—that is, our persistent inclination toward sin, which we have from birth—that generates those sinful attitudes and actions begins to fight back. Romans 7:14–25 helps us understand this internal conflict with the flesh in a helpful way, because it describes the experience of a growing Christian who is continually discovering the depths of sin still present in his or her life. Many Bible students will disagree with that last sentence. In fact, this passage of Scripture has been something of an exegetical battleground for centuries. Pages have been written by capable and godly people presenting other views and rejecting the view to which I subscribe. This is not the place, however, to discuss the various interpretations of Romans 7:14–25. For those who want to pursue this debate,

James Montgomery Boice's expositional commentary on Romans has an excellent, nontechnical discussion of four main interpretations.

Theological giants such as Charles Hodge and John Murray have ably defended the view that Romans 7:14–25 describes the internal conflict between the flesh and the Spirit. And I certainly cannot add anything to their technical arguments. However, I can offer two of the most compelling reasons for seeing the passage as descriptive of the internal conflict with sin that any growing Christian experiences.

First, there is the natural, literary sense of the passage. What would those reading Romans 7:14–25, untutored in familiar theological debates, understand Paul to mean? Would they not assume that Paul is describing himself in his present state at the time he is writing? They might not fully understand what he is saying, but they would assume Paul is describing the reality of his present experience. Paul did not play literary games with his first-century readers. Admittedly, as Peter wrote in 2 Peter 3:16, some things in his letters are hard to understand. But from his point of view, Paul wrote his letters in a straightforward manner to people who were fairly new believers. I believe the first-century Christians in Rome would have assumed Paul was describing his own experience as an illustration of how all believers struggle with the flesh.

The second reason I believe Romans 7:14–25 describes the experience of a growing Christian is that it so accurately reflects the experience of any believer who is intentional about his or her pursuit of a holy and Christ-like life. For the reality is, the more mature we become, the more anguish we experience over the difference between desire and accomplishment in our efforts to put sin to death and to put on Christ-like character.

Early in my Christian life I was exposed to the view that every Christian should "get out of Romans 7 into Romans 8." This view depicts the Romans 7:14–25 person as one who is seeking to live the Christian life in the energy of the flesh, whereas Romans 8 depicts him as living by the power of the Holy Spirit. The Romans 7 person is living a life of spiritual defeat, but the Romans 8 man is living a life of continual victory. This view created great frustration for me because I never seemed to be able to make the transition from Romans 7 to Romans 8.

I could see myself described in Romans 7, but I assumed that was because I was a "defeated" Christian. Then gradually I came to the conviction that a person never does get out of Romans 7 in the sense that he or she no longer struggles with the flesh. God providentially brought me into contact with the works of the older Reformed writers who reinforced my newly developed conviction. This was a great liberating experience. I found I could deal with the reality of the Romans 7 conflict when I realized it was the normal experience of people who are sincere and intentional about spiritual growth.

Again, the reality for every believer is that the more one grows in Christian maturity, the sharper this conflict becomes. The more we understand the perfect will of God, the more we see how far short we come in obeying it. And we should keep in mind that we are not only to joyously obey the moral will of God, but we are to graciously submit to the providential will of God—that is, to the circumstances, whether good or bad, that he brings or allows into our lives.

One of the most difficult precepts to obey of the moral will of God is found in 1 Thessalonians 5:18: "Give thanks in all circumstances, for this is the will of God in Christ Jesus for you." That this is a moral command is shown by Paul's identical expression in chapter 4, verse 3 where he writes: "For this is the will of God, your sanctification: that you abstain from sexual immorality." It is God's moral will that we abstain from immorality, and it is also God's moral will that we give thanks in all circumstances.

Now, most Christians readily understand it is God's will that we abstain from sexual immorality. That command seems relatively easy to obey, especially if we focus on the act and not the thoughts of the heart. But to give thanks in difficult circumstances is an altogether different matter. Oftentimes I find myself giving thanks not wholeheartedly but as a sheer act of the will. But I don't think that is really giving thanks. Recently, in a situation that did not turn out the way I had hoped it would, I said to God: "Father, I give you thanks for the way this has turned out, but I am disappointed." Then the thought came to me that Jesus would not have been disappointed. Jesus so perfectly trusted his Father's providential care of his life that he freely submitted to whatever circumstances came his way.

Now I know and have taught numerous times that nothing happens to us that God does not ordain; that a sparrow cannot fall to the ground apart from his will and that we are of more value than many sparrows (Matt. 10:29–31). This being true then, why do I not give thanks genuinely and joyously? Why do I not accept the fact that my infinitely wise and loving Father has ordained these circumstances for my good? It is because "when I want to do right [that is, joyously give thanks] evil [that is, the desire for my own agenda] lies close at hand" (Rom. 7:21). The flesh in the form of my own desires is often in conflict with the will of God.

I have deliberately chosen to use my recent experience with 1 Thessalonians 5:18 because it illustrates a point. The more we grow in Christian character, the more deeply God digs into our inner being to expose the works of the flesh that are still there. As a young Christian, the command of 1 Thessalonians 5:18 was not an issue for me. There were more obvious desires of the flesh I had to contend with. Now, after fifty-seven years of being a Christian, I realize that God is not content merely dealing with the surface sins. He wants to take on the more subtle issues. So often I now find true the words of Romans 7:18b, "For I have the desire to do what is right but not the ability to carry it out." I have the desire to give thanks in all circumstances but not the ability to do it wholeheartedly, without reserve.

That's because the desires of the flesh, in the form of my agenda, are against the desires of the Spirit (Gal. 5:17). It is because the passions of the flesh still wage war against my soul (1 Pet. 2:11).

Someone has stated that sanctification (that is, spiritual growth) is more often characterized by desire than by performance. I believe that is true of the person in Romans 7. He wants to do what is right. He delights in the law of God. But evil lies close at hand, waging war against the law of his mind (vv. 21–23). I hasten to add, however, that these verses in Romans 7 are descriptive only of a person who is sincerely and intentionally seeking to grow in Christ-like character. The person who is complacent about his Christian experience and is not concerned about remaining sin in his life should find no comfort in this passage of Scripture. Romans 7 does not provide an excuse for tolerating sin but simply describes the experience of one who does not tolerate it but rather struggles against it.

How then does the person who is sincere and intentional about dealing with sin in his or her life handle the tension and frustration that seem so pervasive in verses 14–25? Is there no hope of ever experiencing the joy of the Christian life? Yes, there is. And Paul gives us two reasons to rejoice.

First, there is the confident expectation of future deliverance. In verses 24–25 Paul looks forward to the day when he will be delivered from this body of death. Paul knows that when that day arrives, he will be forever free from the struggle with indwelling sin. At last his experience will exactly coincide with his standing of perfect righteousness in Christ.

The second reason we can rejoice in the midst of our struggle is because of the truth of the gospel, which actually brackets the whole chapter of Romans 7. In verses 1–6, Paul teaches us both by analogy and directly that we have "died to the law through the body of Christ" (v. 4). That is, through our union with Christ in his death we have died to the curse and condemning power of the law. We have died to the reign of the law in our lives. It can no longer pronounce us guilty because Christ has already borne our guilt on the cross.

Then in Romans 8:1, Paul assures us that "there is therefore now no condemnation for those who are in Christ Jesus." So, Romans 7:4 and 8:1 say essentially the same thing: God does not look on our struggles against indwelling sin with an attitude of condemnation and judgment because the condemning power of his law has been forever dealt with by Christ.

So in the midst of our struggle with indwelling sin, we must continually keep our focus on the gospel. We must always go back to the truth that even in the face of the fact that so often "I do not do the good that I want, but the evil I do not want is what I keep on doing" (v. 19), there is no condemnation. God no longer counts our sin against us (Rom. 4:8). Or, to say it another way, God wants us to find our primary joy in our objectively declared justification, not in our subjectively per-ceived sanctification. Regardless of how much progress we make in our pursuit of holiness, it will never come close to the absolute perfect righteousness of Christ that is ours through our union with him in his life and death.

So we should learn to live with the discomfort of the justified life. We should accept the fact that as still-growing Christians we will always be dissatisfied with our sanctification. But at the same time, we should remember that in Christ we are justified. We are righteous in him. There is the familiar play on the word "justification" that it means "just as if I'd never sinned." But there is another way of saying this that is even better—justification means "just as if I'd always obeyed." That's the way we stand before God: clothed in the imputed righteousness of Jesus Christ. And that's the way we can live with the discomfort of the justified life.

Finding True Peace with God

BY W. ROBERT GODFREY

Therefore, since we have been justified through faith, we have peace with God through our Lord Jesus Christ, through whom we have gained access by faith into this grace in which we now stand. (Rom. 5:1–2)

After Paul presents his most detailed discussion of justification in Romans 3 and 4, he concludes that we therefore have peace with God. But what is that peace? In some parts of the world, peace may mean the end of armed conflict even though the old hatreds and armaments remain. This situation is not so much peace as a cease-fire. Or peace may be referred to a situation like the American sector in Berlin after World War II. Fighting had stopped, arms laid down, and hatred abandoned (by Germans thankful that they were not in the Russian sector), but only devastation and rubble marked the reality of life after the peace. Paul has something much more positive in mind when he thinks of peace in Romans 5:1. He thinks of the "way of peace," a phrase from Isaiah 59:8, which he quotes in Romans 3:17. For Isaiah the way of peace stands for holiness, love, justice, integrity, truth, contentment, and righteousness. It is the straight path of life with a loving and redeeming God in contrast to the crooked path of the wicked.

In the immediate context of the Epistle to the Romans, Paul juxtaposed peace with the just punishment for sin (Rom. 3:25) that God in his wrath (Rom. 4:15) would visit upon the wicked (Rom. 4:5). The reality of sin and the reality of God's justice and holiness are essential elements of a Christian outlook on the world. One of the tragedies of so much contemporary church life is that the truth about the holiness of God and his wrath against sin has all but disappeared from view. In an effort to "connect" with contemporary non-Christians, the church has given much of its energy to teaching self-acceptance. The implication is that the great human need is to have peace with yourself. But such a view is far from both the biblical revelation and from true Christianity.

In a Christian view of reality, the first function of the law in a fallen world is to teach the sinfulness of sin (Rom. 3:20) and that those lost in sin do not know the way of peace (Rom. 3:17). The peace in which Paul rejoiced is the peace of sin covered, wrath averted, and justice satisfied so that believing sinners are fully reconciled to God as their loving, heavenly Father in Jesus Christ.

Paul's reflections on peace as the fruit of justification may well depend in part on Isaiah 57. Of the contrite, God says, "I have seen his [sinful] ways, but I will heal him; I will guide him and restore comfort to him, creating praise on the lips of the mourners of Israel. Peace, peace, to those far and near" (Isa. 57:18–19). But of the wicked, "'There is no peace,' says my God'" (Isa. 57:21). The wicked are those who are indifferent to the covenant of the true God and have formed a false righteousness for themselves. God says of them, "Whom have you so dreaded and feared that you have been false to me, and have neither remembered me nor pondered this in your hearts? Is it not because I have long been silent that you do not fear me? I will expose your righteousness and your works, and they will not benefit you" (Isa. 57:11–12).

OBJECTIVE AND SUBJECTIVE PEACE WITH GOD

In commenting on Romans 5, John Calvin explained this peace as the believer's "serenity of conscience, which originates from the awareness of having God reconciled to himself." Notice how Calvin has highlighted the objective and subjective dimensions of the peace. Objectively, peace with God means that God is in fact reconciled to us because of the saving work of Christ. Subjectively, peace with God means that we come to know that God is reconciled to us and that knowledge brings us serenity in our consciences that would otherwise accuse and condemn us. The union of these objective and subjective elements is the glorious peace enjoyed by the children of God.

On the objective side, Jesus has done everything for us to win us that reconciliation with God. Jesus fulfilled the law, not just for himself, but also for us so that our reconciliation means that we stand before God with all of Christ's law-keeping reckoned to our account. Jesus bore the penalty for our sins on the cross so that he has propitiated the wrath of God and expiated our sins. Jesus imputes both his active and passive obedience to his own. As Calvin put it, "When, however, we come to Christ, we first find in him the exact righteousness of the Law, and this also becomes ours by imputation."

On the subjective side, such serenity or peace is missed, Calvin argues, by two sorts of persons. The first are those whose consciences are still filled with fear and a sense of God's anger with them as sinners. "No one will stand without fear before God, unless he relies on free reconciliation, for as long as God is judge, all men must be filled with fear and confusion . . . wretched souls are always uneasy, unless they rest in the grace of Christ." Such people either do not understand the work of Christ in its fullness and completeness, or they have not rightly understood the implications of the gospel for themselves. The former are filled with fear because they think they have failed to augment what is lacking in the work of Christ. These people demean Christ, thinking to add their works to his without realizing that such an addition is always a subtraction (like adding a mustache to the *Mona Lisa*). The latter do not grasp that the full benefit of Christ's work is theirs by faith alone. They are like hypochondriacs who, although healthy, do not enjoy their healthy state.

The second sort, according to Calvin, are those who see no danger for themselves. "This serenity is possessed neither by the Pharisee, who is inflated by a false confidence in his works, nor by a senseless sinner, who, since he is intoxicated with the pleasure of his vices, feels no lack of peace....Peace with God is opposed to the drunken security of the flesh." Here again are two kinds of people. The former actually are secure in believing that their works are good enough to gain them some claim on the divine goodness. They utterly fail to know that even our best works are flawed in the sight of God. The latter—perhaps the majority in our world—have no sense at all of any danger from the wrath of God. They are like the dying man who, when asked if he had made his peace with God, responded that he did not know they had quarreled.

FAITH RIGHTLY UNDERSTOOD

The only true antidote to either fear or self-satisfaction is faith. Faith is that trust in Christ and his work, which looks away from all the valid grounds in ourselves for fear and from all the vain flattery of self-satisfaction. Faith alone looks to Christ alone, and Christ alone justifies those who have faith alone.

The tragedy of contemporary evangelical fuzziness on—or betrayal of—the Protestant doctrine of justification should now be clear. Justification is not some irrelevant squabble over technical bits of theology, nor is it a doctrine subordinate to Christian cooperation and activity. The doctrine of justification determines the way in which we understand the gospel we have to preach, the legitimate bounds of cooperation, and the motivation for good works. Where the biblical doctrine of justification is not kept pristine, true peace with God is forfeited.

Again, we can listen to Calvin as he puts the objective and subjective dimensions of our peace with God together: "We see now how the righteousness of faith is the righteousness of Christ. When, therefore, we are justified, the efficient cause is the mercy of God, Christ is the substance (*materia*) of our justification, and the Word, with faith, the instrument. Faith is therefore said to justify, because it is the instrument by which we receive Christ, in whom righteousness is communicated to us." Here is the true peace that the world needs and that Christ gives.

Holiness:
God's Work
or Ours?

BY HAROLD L. SENKBEIL

T he biblical terms *sanctify* and *sanctification* are from the same word family as *holy* and *holiness*. The rich tapestry of the biblical language of holiness contains but one single golden strand woven throughout: the absolute sinlessness and transcendent purity of God the Holy Trinity. God alone is holy in himself, and therefore from God himself all holiness must proceed; apart from him nothing is holy. Therefore God sends forth his Holy Spirit so that by his grace we believe his holy Word. That Word (also in its sacramental forms) is the means the Holy Spirit uses to *sanctify* us—to make us holy—within the fellowship of the Holy Christian Church, which is the communion of *saints*, or holy people.

As long as sanctification is seen as primarily in the arena of human morality, the heart of sanctification is lost. True, sanctification does effect a change in morality, but sanctification in itself is a question not of human morality, but divine purity. Once sinners are purified by God's divine grace, they live lives that reflect God's own holiness.

BORROWED HOLINESS

This is absolutely vital. If you and I as sinners are to spend eternity in the presence of a holy God, we must share in his holiness: "Strive for...the holiness ✔ without which no one will see the Lord" (Heb. 12:14). The truth is, since the fall of Adam every human being is excluded from the presence of God except one: God's own sinless and holy Son. We have no holiness in this world apart from Jesus Christ, the Holy One of God. Believers borrow their holiness from ✔ him by faith. Sanctification therefore comes as good news; it is gift language, for it means our cleansing and purification through the forgiveness of our sins for Jesus' sake. All who are baptized into Christ have put on Christ by faith, together with the holiness that belongs to him, "that we may share in his holiness" (Heb. 12:10). Sanctification is therefore just as much a gift as is justification.

There is a link between faith and life, between justification and sanctification, between salvation and holy living. And that link is Christ. He "has become for us wisdom from God—that is, our righteousness, holiness and redemption" (1 Cor. 1:30). We have no life to live as Christians that is not given by God the Father, earned by God the Son, and bestowed by God the Holy Spirit. Therefore our focus is always on Jesus Christ, God incarnate in human flesh. Because he is our *redemption*, or atoning sacrifice for sin, he is also our *righteousness*, or perfection before God. And because he is our righteousness/redemption, he is also our *holiness*, or sanctification. With St. Paul, we have one Christ-centered confession: "For me to live is Christ" (Phil. 1:21). In this way the bondage to our private emotions is broken, and we live holy lives in perfect freedom "outside of ourselves."

OUR PART?

One of the most ancient and persistent Christian heresies (viz. Pelagianism and semi-Pelagianism) is that human beings have a role to play in their own salvation. In its most blatant form this heresy claims that Christ's sacrifice is not sufficient to save, but that we must place our own good works into the balance to give us favorable standing before God. Its subtle form seems more attractive: God does all the work in justification, but we finish this work by our sanctification. We may be declared right by God's gracious judicial decree through faith in Christ alone, but then it is up to us to perform the works of love and obedience that true holiness requires. This error makes justification merely the first stage of sanctification. God gets us going on the path of holiness and we continue. God starts and we finish. God has his part and we have ours, so the thinking goes.

But the life we live "in the body" we live by faith in the Son of God who loved us and gave himself for us. We have no life to live apart from the life he bestows by faith. And this faith itself is a gift from God, not of works, lest any man should boast (Eph. 2:9). We are therefore "God's workmanship, created in Christ Jesus to do good works, which God prepared in advance for us to do" (Eph. 2:10). Christian salvation (or justification) and Christian living (or sanctification) are but two aspects of one divine reality: the life bestowed in Jesus Christ. Such life is received by faith. And Holy Scripture declares that faith is God's work from beginning to end: "[I am] confident of this, that he who began a good work in you will carry it on to completion until the day of Christ Jesus" (Phil. 1:6).

OF THE MAKING OF MANY BOOKS

This scriptural teaching is sadly missing in the popular Christian literature of our day. Religious best-sellers focus on the sanctified life, but precious little gospel is contained in these books. What gospel we do find is couched in command language, not motivation language. The books are essentially "how to" lists for the Christian life, what to do and not to do in order to make sense out of the complex world in which we live. The issues of modern life are not examined in light of the good news, but almost exclusively in light of the proscriptions and prescriptions of moral imperatives.

If the modern Christian's dilemma stems from living in an antagonistic culture, then we can profitably learn from the New Testament. Here the apostles were delineating a "lifestyle" for Christians who lived in a world completely at odds with everything they stood for. As we look to the letters of the New Testament, we find many statements describing what the new life in Christ means for everyday stresses and strains. Never, however, do these statements of law stand on their own. Always they are undergirded by the life-giving and empowering gospel of Jesus Christ.

Life for the apostles is not viewed merely as a complex chain of obstacles to overcome by practicing a long list of commands God has prescribed for every contingency. The hostility we encounter in this world cannot be chalked up to the quirks of the human mind. Rather, the New Testament recognizes one sinister enemy behind all of the sins and turmoil of life, both internal and external. He is Satan, the father of lies (John 8:44), the ruler of darkness (Eph. 6:12), the one who accuses God's people in his presence day and night (Rev. 12:10). God's perfect creation has been invaded by this evil adversary, and he can now be called the prince of this world (John 14:30).

Entering this enemy-occupied world, Jesus Christ has assumed human flesh to deal with Satan on his own turf (Gal. 4:5). In the body of his flesh, he has made satisfaction for the sins of the whole world and has defeated the devil by his death and resurrection (Col. 2:14–15). To all who believe in him, he promises everlasting life (John 11:26). Those who trust in him are credited with his very holiness (2 Cor. 5:21). Drawing on this faith relationship, there is light and life in this world of darkness and death (John 1:4).

ONE FOCUS

No wonder the apostles were always framing their description of the new life in Christ in the context of Christ's death and resurrection on their behalf. In everything they had to tell the faithful about living the Christian life, they had one focus and one focus only: "I resolved to know nothing while I was with you except Jesus Christ and him crucified" (1 Cor. 2:2). The entire life of Christian service should be viewed as Christ's action being carried out in the life of the believer: "I have been crucified with Christ and I no longer live, but Christ lives in me. The life I live in the body, I live by faith in the Son of God, who loved me and gave himself for me" (Gal. 2:20).

The difference is striking. Most of the evangelical world puts the spotlight on the Christian's action; the New Testament focuses on Christ's action.

CONTACT WITH GOD

The central attraction of the evangelical movement is not its doctrine of the renewed life in itself, but rather how that renewed life provides demonstrable proof of the reality of God and his action in the world. Carter Lindberg has described the current American scene very well: "The credibility of the church rests on the changed lives of its people, thus only the praise-filled experience of God's presence and power is the answer to today's experience of insecurity and uncertainty. The depersonalization of contemporary life in the midst of materialism and secularism disposes persons to search for a personal experience of reality."[1]

There is another alternative. Rather than seeking the reality of God in our own experience, the Bible directs us to find assurance in the historic events of God's intervention in this world in the person and life of his Son. The basis of our knowledge about God and his living, vibrant reality is not in our experience, but in the experience of Jesus on the cross. There he faced the wrath of the Father and made satisfaction for the sins of the whole world. In his triumphant resurrection, there is validation of his entire saving work. In the word of his gospel, we have no mere static facts about events of history, but the actual means by which people of every age may be brought into genuine contact with the saving work of Christ. "It [the gospel] is the power of God for the salvation of everyone who believes" (Rom. 1:16).

THE POWER FOR SANCTIFICATION

Current evangelical literature—with its myriad of principles, warm folksy illustrations, and down-to-earth advice—presents the power for the new life as a combination of man's work and God's work: Sure, God saves me by grace, but then he expects me to save myself with his help! With his Spirit he gives me the power I need to get started, but then it's up to me. By following his principles and continuing in close fellowship with him and my fellow believers, I will be inspired to produce the kind of life that is pleasing to him. Spectacular power is available; all I have to do is reach out and grab it!

DO-IT-YOURSELF CHRISTIANS?

Thus we see that self-assertion raises its ugly head. Pride is deeply ingrained in the human nature. No one likes to be told he can't do something; in fact, each of us enjoys taking credit for his or her accomplishments. So also when it comes to the Christian faith. There is something deep within us that rebels when Scripture reminds us that there is nothing we can do to save ourselves: "For it is by grace you have been saved, through faith—and this is not from yourselves, it is the gift of God—not by works, so that no one can boast" (Eph. 2:8-9).

Similarly, we do not like to hear that God himself is the driving power in our life of sanctification: "For we are God's workmanship, created in Christ Jesus to do good works, which God prepared in advance for us to do" (Eph. 2:10). True, Scripture does speak of the activity of the Christian in performing works of love: "Continue to work out your salvation with fear and trembling." At the same time, however, we are reminded that the power for the sanctified life is not our own: "For it is God who works in you to will and to act according to his good purpose" (Phil. 2:12-13).

A PACKAGE DEAL

Justification (receiving God's righteousness) and sanctification (sharing in God's holiness) are to be clearly separated theologically, but not essentially. Like the putting the proverbial cart before the horse, putting sanctification before justification is an affront to God's grace and a stumbling block to faith. Holding to justification without sanctification leads nowhere, for "faith without works is dead" (James 2:26). No one setting out on a journey in a horse-drawn cart hitches the cart in front of the horse, nor does he shoot the horse. Together they make a unit. Yet clearly the horse has to come first and provide the power if there is to be any forward movement! As one Lutheran theologian observes:

> Sanctification describes the same reality as does justification but describes the justified Christian's relationship to the world and society. Justification and sanctification are not two separate realities, but the same reality viewed from the different perspectives of God and man. From the perspective of God the reality of the Christian is totally passive and non-contributory as it receives Christ only. From the perspective of the world, the same reality never ceases in its activity and tirelessly performs all good works.[2]

Thus when speaking about the power for the sanctified life, we dare never stop speaking about Christ. St. Paul put it this way: "For I resolved to know nothing while I was with you except Jesus Christ and him crucified" (1 Cor. 2:2). The person and work of the crucified Lord is the sum total of our message. He is all in all: "our righteousness, our sanctification, and our redemption" (1 Cor. 1:30). No wonder, then, that Luther could write, "Having been justified by grace, we then do good works, yes, Christ himself does all in us."[3]

THE SIGN OF JONAH

In the sixteenth chapter of Matthew, we have a remarkable sequence of events that helps us understand how God operates through the cross of his Son in direct opposition to every human expectation.

The Pharisees and Sadducees speak for all of us, asking Jesus to prove his identity (v. 1). We all would like to know where in the world God is, and we would like him to make himself perfectly and unmistakably evident. Jesus, however, makes it clear that there will be no miraculous evidence given. The only evidence will be the "sign of Jonah" (v. 4). The strange three-day sea journey of the Old Testament prophet in the fish's stomach was really a picture of the three-day burial of Jesus. Jesus makes the extraordinary claim that people would be able to see who he was when his lifeless body was placed into a tomb for three days. To ask for any more proof than his death is foolhardy and dangerous; it is following the teachings ("yeast") of the Pharisees and Sadducees (vv. 5–12).

CHURCH GROWTH

When Peter made his glowing confession that Jesus was "the Christ, the Son of the living God" (v. 16), Jesus explained that Peter had not arrived at this convic-tion by human ingenuity. God the Father had revealed it to him.

Whenever people come to faith, it is always on God's initiative. Jesus makes it clear that this is the permanent pattern for the growth of his church; he himself will build it as the Father brings people to confess that he is Christ and God (vv. 18–19).

THE SATANIC PITFALL

Immediately after Peter's confession of faith, Jesus begins to explain what his saving work includes: first, torture at the hands of the power structure in Jerusalem, then execution and, only after that, resurrection (v. 21). Peter is horrified. "This shall never happen to you!" he exclaims (v. 22).

What Jesus has to say to Peter at this point stands for all time as a clear condemnation of every effort to find God through human reason and speculation: "Out of my sight, Satan!...You do not have in mind the things of God, but the things of men" (v. 23). The "things of men" always run directly opposite to the "things of God." The things of men focus on glory and power; the things of God center in weakness and the cross. Human eyes are always on the heights; God's eyes are always on the depths. "God chose the foolish things of the world to shame the wise; God chose the weak things of the world to shame the strong. He chose the lowly things of this world and the despised things—and the things that are not—to nullify the things that are, so that no one may boast before him" (1 Cor. 1:27–28).

Where in the world is God? We want to know. We all want to know. The yeast of the Pharisees and Sadducees is still with us, prodding us to look for God in the experiences of our mind and heart. But we have to let God be God. We have to let him speak where he has promised to speak to us: from the cross of Jesus, his Son!

THE REAL PROBLEM

Most people think that the human dilemma is that our lives are out of adjustment; we don't meet God's expectations. Salvation then becomes a matter of rearranging our priorities and adjusting our lifestyle to correspond with God's will. In its crassest form, this error leads people to think they earn their own salvation. More often in today's evangelical world, the error has a more subtle disguise: armed with forgiveness through Jesus, people are urged to practice the techniques and principles Christ gave to bring their lifestyle back into line.

It is certainly true that sinful lives are out of adjustment. We are all in need of the Spirit's sanctifying power. But that comes only after our real problem is solved. Sins are just the symptom; our real dilemma is death.

GOD'S FINAL SOLUTION

God warned Adam and Eve that the knowledge of evil came with a high price tag: "When you eat [of the tree of the knowledge of good and evil] you will surely die"

(Gen. 2:17). Our first parents wanted to be like God and were willing to pay the price. And we are still paying the price: "the wages of sin is death" (Rom. 6:23); "in Adam all die" (1 Cor. 15:22); "you were dead in your transgressions and sins" (Eph. 2:1).

The real problem we all face is death. Physical death, to be sure. But ultimately and most horribly, spiritual death—being cut off from God forever. And everyone must die. You can either die alone or die in Jesus.[4]

In his death, Jesus Christ swallowed up our death and rose again triumphantly to take all of the teeth out of the grave. In the promise of the resurrection, death loses its power. When we die with Jesus, we really live!

WANTED: DEAD AND ALIVE!

There is no sidestepping death. Everyone must die. It is the basic human dilemma; but the cross is God's great answer to our predicament. We need not die alone. Jesus long ago died in our place, and that means that every baptized Christian dies in Jesus. "Don't you know," St. Paul wrote, "that all of us who were baptized into Christ Jesus were baptized into his death?" (Rom. 6:3). Far from being some mere symbol of our dedication to Jesus, holy baptism is the God-appointed means of planting the cross of Jesus Christ squarely in the midst of our lives.

In our baptism Christ takes us in his arms, sins and all, and carries us into his own tomb to die with him. Death is always frightening. But this death is different, for when you die with Jesus, you also live with him. "If we have been united with him in his death, we will certainly also be united with him in his resurrection" (Rom. 6:5).

That means that if we die in Jesus through our baptism, we also live in Jesus; a resurrection takes place. The difference is that we have died and risen along with Christ: "We were therefore buried with him through baptism into death in order that, just as Christ was raised from the dead through the glory of the Father, we too may live a new life" (Rom. 6:4).

After our burial with Christ in our baptism, we are no longer the same person in God's sight. Our sins have been left behind in his tomb—the one place in all the universe that the Father will not look. And we have a new life through faith in him; it is the risen life of Jesus Christ! "For we know that our old self was crucified with him so that the body of sin might be rendered powerless, that we should no longer be slaves to sin—because anyone who has died has been freed from sin. Now if we died with Christ, we believe that we will also live with him" (Rom. 6:6–8).

THROUGH DEATH TO LIFE

So we see that the cross of Jesus is far more than a nice decoration or a theological concept. In fact, it is the central hinge around which all of faith revolves. At the cross the hidden God opened up his very heart for all to see. In the death of Jesus, the God-Man, with eyes of faith we see most clearly the Father's love. Baptized into that death, the cross takes on a whole new dimension. Now we can see that the only route to life is through death. And death is not to be feared, if it is the death of Jesus—for his death brings life!

That is the hardest thing to learn. We are always trying to avoid hardship, pain, and death. Yet the cross of Jesus reveals to us that the only life worth living is a life that is given through death—the death of Jesus. There is no getting around the cross of Christ; the Christian life is always a life under the cross. But the way of the cross is the way to life. Rather than fleeing from suffering and pain, Jesus invites us to take up our cross and follow him. The only life we have to lose is counterfeit; the life we gain is the real thing—it is the life he lives through us!

Holiness Wars: The Antinomianism Debate

BY MICHAEL S. HORTON

D uring a time of intense controversy and division within Reformed ranks, the English Puritan Richard Sibbes said that "factions breed factions." We are called to the peace *and* purity of the church, but when is the concern for peace a crutch for compromise, and when does our appeal to the church's purity become a cloak for own pride and dogmatism?

Of course, we all say that we should find our unity around primary truth, but I know of no historical debate in which a partisan advocated schism in the name of "secondary matters." Repeatedly these days, I hear church leaders dismiss important age-old debates because they are not "gospel issues," as if we had not been commanded by our Lord to "teach them everything I have commanded you." At the same time, some of the most divisive issues in our churches today concern matters not addressed clearly in God's Word.

One issue, however, that is clearly addressed in Scripture is sanctification: the work of the Spirit through his Word in uniting us to Christ and giving us the grace to grow up into Christ, bearing the fruit of the Spirit. Given the centrality of justification to the Reformation debate, it is not surprising that Reformed, Lutheran, and other evangelical bodies are crystal clear in their confessions and catechisms on this point. In some circles, though, it is wrongly assumed in practice that our confessions aren't quite as clear or as emphatic on sanctification. Reformation theology is great in defining the gospel, but when it comes to the Christian life, we need to supplement it with healthy doses of more "spiritual" or "practical" writers such as Thomas à Kempis, the Pietist Philipp Jacob Spener, John Wesley, or their contemporary voices.

In my view, this would be a tragic conclusion to draw. Before I make that case, however, it's important to define the elephant in the room: *antinomianism*. After all, it's one of those labels often thrown around carelessly today, as in previous eras. After defining it, I'll offer some contemporary reflections by drawing on the rich summary of Reformed teaching on sanctification in the Reformed and Lutheran confessions. In conclusion, I will discuss sanctification and its relationship to the gospel.

DEFINING ANTINOMIANISM(S)

Literally "against law," antinomianism is the view that the moral law summarized in the Ten Commandments is no longer binding on Christians. More generally, antinomianism may be seen as characteristic of human rebellion against any external authority. In this sense, ironically, we are by nature antinomians and legalists since the Fall: rejecting God's command, while seeking to justify ourselves by our own criteria. The modern age is especially identified by the demand for freedom from all constraints. "Be true to yourself" is the modern creed. The rejection of any authority above the self, including obvious biblical norms, is as evident in some denominations as in the wider culture. Antinomianism may also be understood in relation to its opposite, *neonomianism*, which is the view that the gospel is basically just a new law presenting new requirements for the Christian life, even necessary to win God's favor.

In technical terms, however, antinomianism has referred historically more to theory than to practice. For the most part, few of those suspected of this heresy have been charged with dissolute lives, although the concern is that an error in doctrine will inevitably work itself out practically. One of the best summaries of the different varieties of antinomianism is offered by J. I. Packer in his *Concise Theology* (Tyndale House, 2001):

(1) "Dualistic Antinomianism," associated with Gnosticism, treats the body (and its actions) as insignificant;

(2) "Spirit-centered Antinomianism" views the inner promptings of the Spirit as sufficient apart from the external Word;

(3) "Christ-centered Antinomianism" "argues that God sees no sin in believers, because they are in Christ, who kept the law for them, and therefore what they actually do makes no difference, provided that they keep believing";

(4) "Dispensational Antinomianism" denies that in the "church age," believers are obligated to the moral law; and

(5) "Situationist Antinomianism" teaches that love is the only rule and that duties (not just their application) will therefore vary according to circumstance.

Now, it is most common to hear the term *antinomianism* whenever there is a perceived under-emphasis on the pursuit of holiness in Christian living.

ANTINOMIANISM AND REFORMATION CONFESSIONS

While there have been some true-blue antinomians in church history, the charge is often made by those tilting in a more neonomian direction against faithful, apostolic, evangelical preaching. For example, despite the fact that Lutheran and Reformed churches have gone on record against antinomianism in no uncertain terms, that has not kept them from being accused of holding at least implicitly to antinomian tenets. It is therefore important to appeal directly to the Reformation confessions of faith.

THE LUTHERAN CONFESSION

In his Small Catechism, Luther begins with the Ten Commandments, concluding, "God threatens to punish all that transgress these commandments. Therefore we should dread His wrath and not act contrary to these commandments. But He promises grace and every blessing to all that keep these commandments. Therefore we should also love and trust in Him, and gladly do [zealously and diligently order our whole life] according to His commandments." Settling the controversies in its own circles, the Lutherans confess in the Formula of Concord (1577):

> For especially in these last times it is no less needful to admonish men to Christian discipline [to the way of living aright and godly] and good works, and remind them how necessary it is that they exercise themselves in good works as a declaration of their faith and gratitude to God, than that the works be not mingled in the article of justification; because men may be damned by an Epicurean delusion concerning faith, as well as by papistic and Pharisaic confidence in their own works and merits. (IV.2)

After affirming the civil use of the law that curbs public vice, and the "elenctic" use of the law (viz., the law that drives sinners to Christ), Lutherans confessing the Formula of Concord defend the "third use": Even after regeneration, Christians are not left to themselves but have the law as a fixed rule to regulate and direct their lives (VI.1). The following conclusions are worth quoting at length:

> We believe, teach, and confess that, although men truly believing [in Christ] and truly converted to God have been freed and exempted from the curse and coercion of the Law, they nevertheless are not on this account without Law, but have been redeemed by the Son of God in order that they should exercise themselves in it day and night [that they should meditate upon God's Law day and night, and constantly exercise themselves in its observance, Ps. 1:2], Ps. 119. . . . We believe, teach, and confess that the preaching of the Law is to be urged with diligence, not only upon the unbelieving and impenitent, but also upon true believers, who are truly converted, regenerate, and justified by faith. (VI.2–3)

> For although they are regenerate and renewed in the spirit of their mind, yet in the present life this regeneration and renewal is not complete, but only begun, and . . . [on account of this] . . . it is needful that the Law of the Lord always shine before them, in order that they may not from human devotion institute wanton and self-elected cults [that they may frame nothing in a matter of religion from the desire of private devotion, and may not choose divine services not instituted by God's Word]; likewise, that the old Adam also may not employ his own will, but may be subdued against his will, not only by the admonition and threatening of the Law,

but also by punishments and blows, so that he may follow and surrender himself captive to the Spirit, 1 Cor. 9:27; Rom. 6:12, Gal. 6:14; Ps. 119:1f ; Heb. 13:21 (Heb. 12:1). (VI.4)

Therefore, though it is sometimes alleged in evangelical circles that Lutherans do not believe in the "third use" of the law to guide the Christian life, the formula that shapes Lutheran theology and preaching rejects as an "error injurious to, and conflicting with, Christian discipline and true godliness" the view that this law is "not to be urged upon Christians and true believers" (VI.8).

THE REFORMED CONFESSION

In the earlier Reformed confessions, the primary goal is to clear the evangelical doctrine of justification from the Roman Catholic (and Anabaptist) charge that it rejects any place for good works, rather than any direct threat of antinomianism within the ranks.

The Heidelberg Catechism begins its "Gratitude" section by asking why we should still do good works if we are justified by grace alone in Christ alone through faith alone. We do so "because Christ by his Spirit is also renewing us ✓ to be like himself, so that in all our living we may show that we are thankful to God for all he has done for us, and so that he may be praised through us. And we do good so that we may be assured of our faith by its fruits, and so that by our godly living our neighbors may be won over to Christ" (Q. 86). Conversion involves repentance as well as faith: dying to the old self and living to Christ (Q. 87–90). What then defines a "good work"? "Only that which arises out of true faith, conforms to God's law, and is done for his glory; and not that which is based on what we think is right or on established human tradition" (Q. 91).

This sets the stage for the catechism's treatment of the Ten Commandments (Q. 92–113). "In this life even the holiest have only a small beginning of this obedience. Nevertheless, with all seriousness of purpose, they do begin to live according to all, not only some, of God's commandments" (Q. 114). The law must still be preached in the church for two reasons: "First, so that the longer we live the more we may come to know our sinfulness and the more eagerly look to Christ for forgiveness of sins and righteousness. Second, so that, while praying to God for the grace of the Holy Spirit, we may never stop striving to be renewed more and more after God's image, until after this life we reach our goal: perfection" (Q. 115).

The same view is found in articles 15–18 of the Church of England's Thirty-Nine Articles. However, the debates of subsequent decades brought refinement to the Reformed confession and finally appeared in sophisticated form in the Westminster Standards of Faith in 1647.

In the Westminster Confession we find the most mature reflection of Reformed churches on these questions. After a remarkably clear statement of justification, the confession treats sanctification and faith, repentance, and good works in chapters 13–16. Again, the Pauline emphasis on sanctification arising necessarily from election, effectual calling, justification, and adoption is evident.

Christ, "by his Word and Spirit," destroys the dominion of sin, weakening and mortifying its desires while quickening and strengthening the new creature in "the practice of true holiness, without which no man shall see the Lord" (13.1). Though "imperfect in this life," there arises "a continual and irreconcilable war, the flesh lusting against the Spirit and the Spirit against the flesh." Nevertheless, by God's grace the saints will prevail (13.2–3).

Good works are those done according to God's law, not human authority, zeal, or pious intention (16.1). They are "the fruits and evidences of a true and lively faith" (16.2). Yet believers' good works are by grace in Christ, through his Word and Spirit, "not at all of themselves" (16.3).

> We cannot by our best works merit pardon or sin, or eternal life at the hand of God... [since even the best works of believers are still] defiled, and mixed with so much weakness and imperfection, that they cannot endure the severity of God's judgment. Notwithstanding, the persons of believers being accepted through Christ, their good works are also accepted in him; not as though they were in this life wholly unblamable and unreprovable in God's sight; but that he, looking upon them in his Son, is pleased to accept and reward that which is sincere, although accompanied with many weaknesses and imperfections. (16.5–7)

Chapter 19, "Of the Law of God," distinguishes clearly between the way the law functions in a covenant of works (promising life for obedience and threatening death for disobedience) and in the covenant of grace.

> Although true believers be not under the law, as a covenant of works, to be thereby justified, or condemned; yet it is of great use to them, as well as to others; in that, as a rule of life informing them of the will of God, and their duty, it directs and binds them to walk accordingly; discovering also the sinful pollution of their nature, hea rts, and lives; so as, examining themselves thereby, they may come to further conviction of, humiliation for, and hatred against sin, together with a clearer sight of the need they have of Christ, and the perfection of his obedience. (19.6)

Expanding on the law/gospel distinction that grounds it, the federal scheme (covenant of works/covenant of grace) is crucial for avoiding legalism as well as antinomianism.

CONFESSIONAL WISDOM FOR CONTEMPORARY DEBATES

I have quoted Lutheran and Reformed confessions at length on this question, at least in part because I sense that in some circles today there is a dangerous tendency to rally around people, forming tribes around particular flags. Unchecked, this leads—as church history teaches us—to slander and schism.

There are several dangers to point out regarding this temptation to follow persons rather than to confess the faith together with saints across various times and places. There are personal idiosyncrasies attached to individuals, no matter how great their insight into God's Word. With a clear conscience, Paul could tell the Ephesian elders that he had fulfilled his office, declaring to them "the whole counsel of God" (Acts 20:27). This is our goal, too. Paul's message came directly from the ascended Christ, and yet his letters reflect the particular controversies, strengths, and weaknesses of the churches he served. His personality and emphases differed at times from those of other apostles, even Peter and James—sometimes to the point of sharp confrontations. Nevertheless, the Spirit brought a sweet unity to the apostolic church as it gathered in a representative synod of "apostles and elders." In solemn assembly in Jerusalem, the whole church received its marching orders for the proper view and treatment of Gentile believers.

How much more, after the death of the apostles, is our Lord's wisdom evident in the representative assemblies of his body? It's interesting that at the Council of Jerusalem not even Peter was given precedence over the body. Not even Athanasius's writings were made binding at Nicaea, and Reformed churches do not subscribe to anything written by Calvin. Jonathan Edwards did not sit at the Westminster Assembly. We are not obliged today to these confessions because of great persons, but because they are great summaries of God's Word.

It can be as difficult for their followers as for prominent preachers and theologians themselves to submit to the consensus of a whole body rather than to promote their own distinctive teachings, emphases, and corrections. Those who were raised in more legalistic and Arminian backgrounds may be prone to confuse every call to obedience as a threat to newly discovered doctrines of grace. The zeal of those who are converted from a life of debauchery or perhaps from a liberal denomination may boil over into legalistic fervor. As at the Jerusalem Council, representatives came to Nicaea, Chalcedon, Torgau, Dort, and Westminster with idiosyncrasies. Yet they had to make their case, participate in restrained debate, and talk *to* each other in a deliberative assembly, rather than *about* each other on blogs and in conversations with their circle of followers. Muting personal idiosyncrasies in favor of a consensus on the teaching of God's Word, these assemblies give us an enduring testimony for our own time. Nothing has changed with respect to how sinners are justified and sanctified. There has been no alteration of God's covenantal law or gospel.

If the growing charges and countercharges of antinomianism and legalism continue to mount in our own circles, may God give us good and godly sense to recover the wisdom of our confessions as faithful summaries of biblical faith and practice. And may the Spirit direct us to the fraternal fellowship of the church's representative assemblies for mutual encouragement and correction.

Does
Justification
Still Matter?

BY MICHAEL S. HORTON

Once upon a time, the label "evangelical" identified those who were committed not only to historic Christianity but to the doctrine of justification by grace alone through faith alone because of Christ alone. In our day, however, that can no longer be taken for granted. Increasingly, evangelical scholarship is challenged by trends in biblical studies (especially the New Perspective on Paul) to abandon the Reformation's understanding of justification. Recent ecumenical rapprochements (such as the Lutheran-Roman Catholic Joint Declaration on Justification and "Evangelicals and Catholics Together") have revised and relativized this key article.[1]

Remarkably, in a book with essays by mainline Protestants (Lutheran and Reformed) and Roman Catholics on justification, the former reject the Reformation doctrine (by appeal to the New Perspective on Paul) while leading Roman Catholic New Testament scholar Joseph Fitzmyer demonstrates the technical accuracy of the Reformation's exegesis of the relevant passages. In *Is the Reformation Over?* leading evangelical scholar Mark Noll seems to be speaking for a lot of conservative Protestants in answering yes.

Outright criticism of the doctrine of justification as it is defined in our Reformed confessions and catechisms has become common even in conservative churches. Although the church courts of these sister denominations have exhibited a heartening solidarity in standing for the confessional position and prosecuting ministers who oppose it, it is tragic that controversies over this cardinal doctrine should arise in our own circles.

Most people in the pew, however, are simply not acquainted with the doctrine of justification. Often, it is not a part of the diet of preaching and church life, much less a dominant theme in the Christian subculture. With either stern rigor or happy tips for better living, "fundamentalists" and "progressives" alike smother the gospel in moralism, through constant exhortations to personal and/or social transformation that keep the sheep looking to themselves rather than looking outside of themselves to Christ. Even in many churches formally committed to Reformation teaching, people may find the doctrine of justification in the back of their hymnal (in the confessions section), but is it really taken seriously in the teaching, preaching, worship, and life of the congregation? The average Christian best-seller or feature article in *Christianity Today* is concerned with "good works"—trends in spirituality, social activism, church growth, and discipleship. However, it's pretty clear that justification is simply not on the radar. Even where it is not outright rejected, it is often ignored. Perhaps the forgiveness of sins and justification are appropriate for "getting saved," but then comes the real business of Christian living—as if there could be any genuine holiness of life that did not arise out of a perpetual confidence that "there is therefore now no condemnation to those who are in Christ Jesus" (Rom. 8:1).

Of course, it's impossible to track down all the reasons for the attitude toward this doctrine that lies at the heart of the gospel itself, but in this essay I will point out a couple of the dominant sources.

CULTURE-CHRISTIANITY AS SELF-HELP MORALISM

Although it has been said in various other ways by the Reformers, it was the early seventeenth-century Reformed theologian J. H. Alsted who identified the doctrine of justification as "the article of a standing or falling church." Yet by the next century, Protestant denominations that had sealed this confession with martyr's blood were gradually surrendering it to various forms of moralism that were rife in the era of the Enlightenment—and in many cases worse than the distortions that provoked the Reformation in the first place. Even in Pietist circles, where a vital faith in Christ was preserved, the scales increasingly tipped in favor of subjective piety and obedience, so that justification was made subordinate to sanctification.

As Arminianism gathered strength, a new legalism (identified by Reformed critics as "neo-nomianism") entered churches formally committed to evangelical doctrine, breeding a suspicion of the preaching of election and justification as a motivation for "antinomianism" (anti-law-ism). After reading William Law's *A Serious Call to a Devout and Holy Life*, John Wesley became convinced that the residual Calvinism in the Church of England stood in the way of a genuine revival of inner piety and committed discipleship. Although he eventually came to embrace the doctrine of justification, he remained concerned that it would lead to license unless it was subordinated to sanctification.

In the American colonies, the Great Awakening, under the leadership of Jonathan Edwards and George Whitefield, heralded the good news of God's justifying grace in Christ. By the Second Great Awakening, however, an antithetical theology became the working theology of many Protestant bodies in the new republic. The church is a society of moral reformers, said its leading evangelist Charles Finney. How could there be any genuine transformation of society if Calvinism were true?

Finney's critics charged him with Pelagianism—the ancient heresy that essentially taught that we are not born inherently sinful and that we are saved by following Christ's moral example. Going well beyond Rome's errors, Finney's *Systematic Theology* explicitly denied original sin and insisted that the power of regeneration lies in the sinner's own hands, rejected any notion of a substitutionary atonement in favor of the moral influence and moral government theories, and regarded the doctrine of justification by an imputed righteousness as "impossible and absurd."[2]

Concerning the complex of doctrines that he associated with Calvinism (including original sin, vicarious atonement, justification, and the supernatural character of the new birth), Finney concluded, "No doctrine is more dangerous than this to the prosperity of the Church, and nothing more absurd." He declared that "a revival is not a miracle" and, in fact, "there is nothing in religion beyond the ordinary powers of nature."[3] Find the most useful methods, "excitements sufficient to induce conversion," and there will be conversion. "A revival will decline and cease," he warned, "unless *Christians are frequently re-converted*."[4] Toward the end of his ministry, as he considered the condition of many who had experienced his revivals, Finney wondered if this endless craving for ever-greater experiences might lead to spiritual exhaustion.[5] His worries were justified. The area where Finney's revivals were especially dominant is now referred to by historians as the "burned-over district," a seedbed of both disillusionment and the proliferation of various cults.[6] Ever since, evangelicalism has been characterized by a succession of enthusiastic movements hailed as "revivals" that have burned out as quickly as they spread. Paul could as easily say today of American Protestantism what he said of his brethren according to the flesh: "I can testify that they have a zeal for God, but it is not according to knowledge. For, being ignorant of the righteousness that comes from God, and seeking to establish their own, they have not submitted to God's righteousness. For Christ is the end of the law so that there may be righteousness for everyone who believes" (Rom. 10:3–4).

There are two religions, says Paul: "The righteousness that is by works" and "the righteousness that is by faith." While the former feverishly pursues its schemes of self-salvation, trying to bring Christ down or raise him up from the dead, as it were, the latter simply receives the word of Christ and rests in it alone (vv. 5–8). "But how are they to call on one in whom they have not believed? And how are they to believe in one of whom they have never heard? And how are they to hear without someone to proclaim him?...So faith comes from what is heard, and what is heard comes through the word of Christ" (v. 17).

It does not seem wide of the mark to regard Finney's theological assumptions as Pelagian and to see that his influence remains with us today, in both mainline and evangelical Protestantism. Dietrich Bonhoeffer saw this clearly in his visit to the United States, describing American religion as "Protestantism without the Reformation."[7] In spite of the influence of a genuinely evangelical witness, the rapid spread of Arminian revivalism, especially in the developing West, proved more effective in producing "results." Doctrine in general, and Calvinism in particular, just got in the way of building a Christian America. "Deeds, not creeds!" has a long pedigree in the movement's history.

Americans are "pull-yourself-up-by-your-own-bootstraps" kind of people anyway. That is what accounts in part for the enormous vitality of American business and industry. It also became a religion. Those who worked their way from rags to riches could hardly be told that before God, at least, they were helpless sinners who needed to be rescued. In today's climate, American Protestantism on the left and the right is committed to Finney's legacy, whether it knows it or not. It can be recognized in the "social gospel" of the left and in the moralistic jeremiads of the right; in the "how-to" pragmatism of the church growth movement and in the vast self-help literature and preaching that have become the diet in the Christian subculture; and in the therapeutic obsession with inner spirituality and social activism one finds in the Emergent movement. Even if the gospel is formally affirmed, it becomes a tool for engineering personal and public life (salvation-by-works), rather than an announcement that God's just wrath toward us has been satisfied and his unmerited favor has been freely bestowed in Jesus Christ.

I say all of this with deep regret at having to say it, because it is the worst thing that can ever be said of a church. Paul spoke sharply to the Corinthians concerning their immorality, but he never questioned whether they were a church. However, when the Galatian church was confusing the gospel of God's free justification in Christ through faith alone, he warned them that they were on the verge of being cut off—excommunicated, "anathema."

And this concern I have expressed is hardly limited to a few grumpy Calvinists and Lutherans. "Self-salvation is the goal of much of our preaching," according to United Methodist bishop William Willimon.[8] Willimon perceives that much of contemporary preaching, whether mainline or evangelical, assumes that conversion is something we generate through our own words and sacraments. "In this respect we are heirs of Charles G. Finney," who thought that conversion was not a miracle but a "'purely philosophical [i.e., scientific] result of the right use of the constituted means.'"

> [W]e have forgotten that there was once a time when evangelists were forced to defend their "new measures" for revivals, that there was once a time when preachers had to defend their preoccupation with listener response to their Calvinist detractors who thought that the gospel was more important than its listeners. I am here arguing that revivals are miraculous, that the gospel is so odd, so against the grain of our natural inclinations and the infatuations of our culture, that nothing less than a miracle is required in order for there to be true hearing. My position is therefore closer to that of the Calvinist Jonathan Edwards than to the position of Finney.[9]

Nevertheless, "The homiletical future, alas, lay with Finney rather than Edwards," leading to the evangelical church marketing guru, George Barna, who writes, "Jesus Christ was a communications specialist. He communicated His message in diverse ways, and with results that would be a credit to modern advertising and marketing agencies....He promoted His product in the most efficient way possible: by communicating with the 'hot prospects.'...He understood His product thoroughly, developed an unparalleled distribution system, advanced a method of promotion that has penetrated every continent, and offered His product at a price that is within the grasp of every consumer (without making the product so accessible that it lost its value)."[10]

The question that naturally arises in the face of such remarks is whether it is possible to say that Jesus made anything new. "Alas," adds Willimon, "most 'evangelistic' preaching I know about is an effort to drag people even deeper into their subjectivity rather than an attempt to rescue them from it." Our real need, whether we feel it or not, is that we systematically distort and ignore the truth. This is why we need "an external word."[11] "So in a sense, we don't discover the gospel, it discovers us. 'You did not choose me but I chose you' (John 15:16)."[12] "The story is *euangelion, good* news, because it is about grace. Yet it is also news because it is not common knowledge, not what nine out of ten average Americans already know. Gospel doesn't come naturally. It comes as Jesus."[13]

The evangelical faith and practice proclaimed in the Scriptures is always unnatural to us. Born in sin, curved in on ourselves, we assume that we are good people who could be better if we just had a good plan, environment, and examples. When visiting people on their deathbeds, it is always disconcerting to encounter lifelong members of confessional Reformed churches express the hope that they have been good enough for God to accept them. We're born Pelagians, trusting in ourselves rather than in God, and this is our default setting even as Christians. That's why we can never assume the gospel; it has to be the staple diet not only for the beginning but for the middle and the end of the Christian pilgrimage. When things fall apart in our personal or corporate faith, the direction is always the same: we fall back on works-righteousness.

Periods of genuine health and vitality are always the consequence of rediscovering the gospel of grace; eras of decline are always associated with the eclipse of the gospel of a one-sided divine rescue in the person and work of Jesus Christ. Since Satan lost the war at Golgotha and the tomb, he has turned his assault to the faith of believers in the gospel and the progress of that gospel to the ends of the earth. He knows our weak spot and he exploits it. If he cannot destroy the church by persecution, he will weaken it through heresy. And Pelagianism—self-salvation in all its forms—is his best-seller. After conducting numerous studies over the last several years with his team, University of North Carolina sociologist Christian Smith concluded that the religion of America's youth can be characterized as "moralistic, therapeutic deism." When we interviewed him for the *White Horse Inn* and *Modern Reformation,* he said there was no difference between the churched and unchurched or even between the unchurched and young people raised in evangelical churches today.

WHO NEEDS JUSTIFICATION?

God justifies the *wicked.* That's pretty radical. It is more radical than the claim that God heals the morally sick or gives grace to those who are willing to cooperate with it or that he rewards those who try to do their best. We don't even have to deny justification outright. It's just irrelevant when we stop asking the most important question. Having trouble with the marriage or the kids? Sure. Not living up to our expectations? Doesn't everybody? Not really getting the most out of life and need some fresh advice? I'm all ears. But we don't care about being "sinners in the hands of an angry God" if we have never encountered a holy God. And if we do not sense a great need, we do not cry out for a great Savior.

While Roman Catholics and Protestants used to debate *how* those born in original sin are saved by grace, these theological categories themselves are becoming replaced across the Roman Catholic-Protestant and liberal-evangelical divides with therapeutic, pragmatic, and consumerist categories that seem to render gospel-speech itself irrelevant. The question "How can I be accepted by a holy God?" is replaced with the quest for self-fulfillment, self-respect, self-esteem, and self-effort. And there are plenty of preachers who will cater to our narcissism, dressing our wound as though it were not serious and telling us how we can have our best life now.

When *God* is no longer a problem for humanity, but a domesticated icon of either an irrelevant transcendence or a usefully immanent source of therapeutic well-being and moral causes, justification becomes an empty symbol. No longer lost, we are more like somewhat dysfunctional but well-meaning victims who simply need "empowerment" and better instructions. Our experience is remote from that of the Israelites assembled at the foot of Mount Sinai when they heard God's terrifying voice and begged for a mediator.

The holiness of God obscured, the sinful human condition is adjusted first to the level of *sins*—that is, to particular acts or habits that require scolding and reform. Weary of browbeating that actually trivializes the sinful condition, the next generation takes a more positive, therapeutic approach, offering "tips for living" that will make life happier, healthier, and more fulfilling. Finally, the vertical dimension is all but lost. That which makes sin *sinful* is the fact that it is first of all an offence against God (Ps. 51:3–5). As a result, it is no longer conceivable that God became flesh to bear his own just wrath. The purpose of the cross is to move us to repentance by showing us how much God loves us (the moral influence theory of the atonement), to display God's justice (the moral government theory), or to liberate the oppressed from unjust social structures (Christus Victor). But the one thing it *cannot* be is the means by which "we have been justified by his blood [and]...saved through him from the wrath of God" (Rom. 5:9).

In fact, in "Justification and Atonement: An Ecumenical Trajectory," mainline Lutheran theologian George Lindbeck explored the inseparable relationship between justification and atonement, concluding that even where the former is formally affirmed, the widespread lack of interest in our outright rejection of traditional atonement language leaves it without sufficient specificity. At least in practice, Abelard's view of salvation by following Christ's example (and the cross as the demonstration of God's love that motivates our repentance) now seems to have a clear edge over Anselm's satisfaction theory of the atonement.

"The atonement is not high on the contemporary agendas of either Catholics or Protestants," Lindbeck surmises. "More specifically, the penal-substitutionary versions (and distortions) of Anselm's satisfaction theory that have been dominant on the popular level for hundreds of years are disappearing."[14] This is as true, he says, for evangelicals as for liberal Protestants.

Those who continued to use the *sola fide* language assumed that they agreed with the Reformers no matter how much, under the influence of conversionist pietism and revivalism, they turned the faith that saves into a meritorious good work of the free will, a voluntaristic decision to believe that Christ bore the punishment of sins on the cross *for me*, for each person individually. Improbable as it might seem given the metaphor (and the Johannine passage from which it comes), everyone is thus capable of being "born again" if only he or she tries hard enough. Thus, with the loss of the Reformation understanding of the faith that justifies itself as God's gift, Anselmic atonement theory became culturally associated with a self-righteousness that was both moral and religious and therefore rather nastier, its critics thought, than the primarily moral self-righteousness of the liberal Abelardians. In time, to move on in our story, the liberals increasingly ceased to be even Abelardian.[15]

Lindbeck writes that "our increasingly feel-good therapeutic culture is antithetical to talk of the cross" and that our "consumerist society has made the doctrine a pariah....A more puzzling feature of this development as it has affected professedly confessional churches is the silence that has surrounded it. There have been few audible protests."[16] Even most contemporary theologies of the cross fit the pattern of Jesus-as-Model, but justification itself is rarely described in accordance with the Reformation pattern even by conservative evangelicals, Lindbeck suggests. Most of them, as has already been indicated, are conversionists holding to Arminian versions of the *ordo salutis*, which are further removed from Reformation theology than was the Council of Trent.[17] "Where the cross once stood is now a vacuum."[18] Evangelicalism today sounds a lot more like Erasmus than Luther.

JUSTIFICATION FEEDS RATHER THAN STARVES THE PASSION FOR GENUINE RENEWAL

Today, a growing number of evangelical theologians and leaders repeat the charge of Pelagius against Augustine, Rome against the Reformers, and Protestant liberalism against evangelicalism: namely, that, in the words of Albert Schweitzer, "There is no place for ethics in the Reformation doctrine of justification." Following evangelical theologians like Stanley Grenz, Brian McLaren and other leaders of the "Emergent Church" movement explicitly challenge *sola fide* as an obstacle to the main point of Christianity: following the example of Jesus. While authentic living brings tribute to the gospel, the former is increasingly *becoming the gospel*.

G. C. Berkouwer's observation is still relevant in our own day when he writes

that "the problem of the renewal of life is attracting the attention of moralists....
Amid numberless chaotic and demoralizing forces is sounded, as if for the
last time, the cry for help and healing, for the re-organization of a dislocated
world. The therapy prescribed perhaps varies, the call for moral and spiritual
re-armament is uniformly insistent....These are the questions we must answer.
For implicit in them is the intent to destroy the connection between justification and sanctification, as well as the bond between faith and sanctification."[19]
Paul relates everything, including sanctification, the problems of ethics, and
ecclesial harmony, to Christ's cross and resurrection.

A pastor once related to me that some of his fellow pastors expressed concern that
too much preaching of grace, especially justification, was dangerous—especially
if it is not immediately followed up with warnings to obedience. Knowing this
pastor pretty well, I was surprised his colleagues were pointing this concern at
him. After all, he is perfectly sound in his theology, and he affirms and preaches
the third use of the law (as guide for Christian obedience). Sometimes we forget
that Paul was accused of being an antinomian—that is, of inviting people to sin
that grace may abound. But instead of retracting the doctrine of justification
(Rom. 3–5) that he knew would provoke that question again, the apostle simply
explained how the gospel is the answer to the tyranny of sin as well as its condemnation (Rom. 6). The gospel of free justification is the source of genuine
sanctification, not its enemy. Yet that is counterintuitive to us. It is gospel-logic,
not the logic of works-righteousness.

Like its native culture, American evangelicalism is activistic. We're used to being
producers and consumers, but not receivers—at least, helpless and ungodly sinners
who must acknowledge their salvation as a free gift, apart from their decision
and effort (Rom. 9:16). Obsessed with what happens with us, evangelical spirituality has for a long time—at least in practice—obscured the good news of that
which has happened once and for all outside of us. Justification may be relevant
for avoiding God's wrath (at least where this is still affirmed), but is it really as
important for the Christian life? Wouldn't it be more helpful and practical to
learn steps for victory over sin in our lives and in our culture?

In *Revisioning Evangelical Theology,* Stanley Grenz argues that evangelicalism is
more a "spirituality" than a "theology," more interested in individual piety than
in creeds, confessions, and liturgies.[20] Experience "determines" doctrine rather
than the other way around.[21] The main point of the Bible is how the stories can
be used in daily living—hence, the emphasis on daily devotions. "Although some
evangelicals belong to ecclesiological traditions that understand the church as in
some sense a dispenser of grace, generally we see our congregations foremost as
a fellowship of believers."[22] We share our journeys (our "testimony") of personal
transformation.[23] Thus, "a fundamental shift in self-consciousness may be under
way" in evangelicalism, "a move from a creed-based to a spirituality-based
identity" that is more like medieval mysticism than Protestant orthodoxy.[24]

"Consequently, spirituality is inward and quietistic,"[25] concerned with combating "the lower nature and the world,"[26] in "a personal commitment that becomes the ultimate focus of the believer's affections."[27] Therefore the origin of faith is not to be attributed to an external gospel but arises from an inner experience. "Because spirituality is generated from within the individual, inner motivation is crucial"—more important than "grand theological statements."[28]

> The spiritual life is above all the imitation of Christ….In general we eschew religious ritual. Not slavish adherence to rites, but doing what Jesus would do is our concept of true discipleship. Consequently, most evangelicals neither accept the sacramentalism of many mainline churches nor join the Quakers in completely eliminating the sacraments. We practice baptism and the Lord's Supper, but understand the significance of these rites in a guarded manner.[29]

In any case, he says, these rites are practiced as goads to personal experience and out of obedience to divine command. "'Get on with the task; get your life in order by practicing the aids to growth and see if you do not mature spiritually,' we exhort. In fact, if a believer comes to the point where he or she senses that stagnation has set in, evangelical counsel is to redouble one's efforts in the task of exercising the disciplines. 'Check up on yourself,' the evangelical spiritual counselor admonishes."[30]

We go to church, he says, not in order to receive "means of grace" but for fellowship, "instruction and encouragement."[31] The emphasis on the individual believer is evident in the expectation to "find a ministry" within the local fellowship.[32] All of this is at odds with an emphasis on doctrine and especially, Grenz adds, an emphasis on "a material and a formal principle"—in other words, *solo Christo* and *sola scriptura*.[33]

When personal and social transformation become the main point of faith and practice, it is no wonder that the line between Roman Catholicism and evangelicalism blurs. For Rome, of course, justification simply *is* sanctification: the moral transformation of the believer. Grace is offered, but we must cooperate with it if we are finally to be accepted and renewed. With its longer and more sophisticated history of cultural influence, Rome's superiority in the arena of world-transformation is apparent. Once our interest in improving ourselves and the world has rendered justification through faith alone irrelevant (or even problematic), why should evangelicals and Mormons remain divided? No longer dividing by doctrine, the "culture Protestantism" of America threatens completely to engulf evangelicalism as it did the mainline denominations. Perhaps the only denominations left with any distinct identity will be the Republican and Democratic parties.

According to the account thus far, justification is not the first stage of the Christian life but the constant wellspring of sanctification and good works. Luther summarizes, "'Because you believe in me,' God says, 'and your faith takes hold of Christ, whom I have freely given to you as your Justifier and Savior, therefore be righteous.' Thus God accepts you or accounts you righteous only on account of Christ, in whom you believe."[34] Whatever other piece of good news (concerning the new birth, Christ's conquest of sin's tyranny and promise to renew us throughout our life, the resurrection of our body and freedom from the presence of sin), much less the useful exhortations we may offer, the announcement Luther here summarizes alone creates and sustains the faith that not only justifies but sanctifies as well.

Good works now may be freely performed for God and neighbors without any fear of punishment or agony over the mixed motives of each act. Because of justification in Christ, even our good works can be "saved," not in order to improve either God's lot or our own, but our neighbor's. As Calvin explains,

> But if, freed from this severe requirement of the law, or rather from the entire rigor of the law, they hear themselves called with fatherly gentleness by God, they will cheerfully and with great eagerness answer, and follow his leading. To sum up: Those bound by the yoke of the law are like servants assigned certain tasks for each day by their masters. These servants think they have accomplished nothing and dare not appear before their masters unless they have fulfilled the exact measure of their tasks. But sons, who are more generously and candidly treated by their fathers, do not hesitate to offer them incomplete and half-done and even defective works, trusting that their obedience and readiness of mind will be accepted by their fathers, even though they have not quite achieved what their fathers intended. Such children ought we to be, firmly trusting that our services will be approved by our most merciful Father, however small, rude, and imperfect these may be....And we need this assurance in no slight degree, for without it we attempt everything in vain.[35]

"Because of justification," adds William Ames, "the defilement of good works does not prevent their being accepted and rewarded by God."[36]

Not only does such a view properly ground works in faith, it also frees believers to love and serve their neighbors apart from the motive of gaining or fear of losing divine favor. It liberates us for a world-embracing activism deeply conscious that although our love and service contribute nothing to God and his evaluation of our persons, they are, however feebly, half-heartedly and imperfectly performed means through which God cares for creation.

Even with the medieval terminology, Reformed theology can maintain the following:

> The renewal is not a mere supplement, an appendage, to the salvation given in justification. The heart of sanctification is the life which feeds on this

justification. There is no contrast between justification as act of God and sanctification as act of man. The fact that Christ is our sanctification is not exclusive of, but inclusive of, a faith which clings to him alone in all of life. Faith is the pivot on which everything revolves. Faith, though not itself creative, preserves us from autonomous self-sanctification and moralism.[37]

The real question, says Berkouwer, is whether justification is sufficient to ground *all* of the blessings communicated in our union with Christ. "The same Catechism [Heidelberg, Lord's Day 24] which denies us even a partial righteousness of our own mentions the earnest purpose with which believers begin to live" according to all the commandments.

> It is this beginning which has its basis solely in justification by faith....It is not true that sanctification simply succeeds justification. Lord's Day 31, which discusses the keys of the kingdom, teaches that the kingdom is opened and shut by proclaiming "to believers, one and all, that, whenever they receive the promise of the gospel by a true faith, all their sins are really forgiven them." This "whenever" illustrates the continuing relevancy of the correlation between faith and justification....The purpose of preaching the ten commandments, too, is that believers may "become the more earnest in seeking remission of sins and righteousness in Christ" [Heidelberg Catechism, Question 115]....Hence there is never a stretch along the way of salvation where justification drops out of sight. Genuine sanctification—let it be repeated—stands or falls with this continued orientation toward justification and the remission of sins.[38]

When we talk about sanctification, we do not leave justification behind. "We are not here concerned with a transition from theory to practice. It is not as if we should proceed from a faith in justification to the realities of sanctification; for we might as truly speak of the reality of justification and our faith in sanctification."[39] Paul teaches that believers are "sanctified in Christ Jesus" (1 Cor. 1:2, 30; 6:11; 1 Thess. 5:23; cf. Acts 20:32; 26:18). As Herman Bavinck puts it, "Many indeed acknowledge that we are justified by the righteousness of Christ, but seem to think that—at least they act as if—they must be sanctified by a holiness they themselves have acquired."[40]

"The apostle Paul," Berkouwer writes, "preaches holiness with repetitive fervor, but in no way does he compromise his unequivocal declaration: 'For I determined not to know anything among you, save Jesus Christ, and him crucified' (1 Cor. 2:2)."

> Not for a moment would he do violence to the implications of that confession. Hence in every exhortation he must be relating his teaching to the cross of Christ. From this center all lines radiate outward—into the life of cities and villages, of men and women, of Jews and Gentiles, into families, youth, and old age, into conflict and disaffection, into immorality and drunkenness. If

we would keep this center, as well as the softer and harder lines flowing from it, in true perspective, we must be thoroughly aware that in shifting from justification to sanctification we are not withdrawing from the sphere of faith. We are not here concerned with a transition from theory to practice. It is not as if we should proceed from a faith in justification to the realities of sanctification; for we might as truly speak of the reality of justification and our faith in sanctification.[41]

Thus Berkouwer finds it "incomprehensible" that the Reformation view could have ever been criticized as having no bearing on sanctification or the life of holiness. It has everything to do with it because it brings everything back to faith in Christ.

Therefore, sanctification is not a human project supplementing the divine project of justification, nor a process of negotiating the causal relations between free will and infused grace, but the impact of God's justifying Word on every aspect of human life. It is time to get the horse before the cart again, first of all so that the church can once more be a place where God's saving work will be known and experienced, and also for that genuine personal and corporate renewal that can only arise out of the continual wonder of the gospel: God's free justification of the ungodly—even Christians.

INTRODUCTION

[1] N. T. Wright, *Justification: God's Plan & Paul's Vision* (Downers Grove: IVP Academic, 2009), 19, 20.

[2] Wright, 112.

[3] Daniel P. Fuller, *Gospel and Law: Contrast or Continuum?* (Grand Rapids: Eerdmans, 1980); *The Unity of the Bible: Unfolding God's Plan for Humanity* (Grand Rapids: Zondervan, 1992).

[4] Fuller, *The Unity of the Bible*, 310 (emphasis added).

[5] Readers may also want to reference Michael Horton, *Introducing Covenant Theology* (Grand Rapids: Baker Books, 2009).

[6] A sophisticated account can be found in Michael S. Horton, *Covenant and Salvation: Union with Christ* (Louisville, KY: Westminster John Knox Press, 2007).

[7] See, for example, Herman Witsius, *The Economy of the Covenants Between God and Man: Comprehending a Complete Body of Divinity* (Charleston, SC: Nabu Press, 2010).

CHAPTER 01

[1] N. T. Wright, *Justification: God's Plan and Paul's Vision* (Downers Grove: IVP, 2009), 12.

[2] With this phrase, probably coined first by E. P. Sanders, each term modifies the other: *covenantal* representing the gracious element, and *nomism* underscoring the obligation to law.

[3] N. T. Wright, *Climax of the Covenant: Christ and the Law in Pauline Theology* (Edinburgh: T & T Clark, 1991), xi, 1.

[4] N. T. Wright, *What Saint Paul Really Said: Was Paul of Tarsus the Real Founder of Christianity?* (Grand Rapids: Eerdmans, 1997), 117.

[5] N. T. Wright, *Paul: In Fresh Perspective* (Minneapolis: Fortress, 2006), 13. With this volume, Wright distances himself in a more general way from the

New Perspective on Paul. He suggests that even the New Perspective has been too interested in a theology of salvation rather than in the ostensibly Pauline interest in transforming society under the lordship of Christ.

[6] Covenant (federal) theology was a way of working out in a more biblical-historical way the distinction between law and gospel. On this, see Michael S. Horton, "Calvin and the Law-Gospel Hermeneutic," *Pro Ecclesia* vol.6 no.1: 27–42; "Law, Gospel, and Covenant: Reassessing Some Emerging Antitheses," *Westminster Theological Journal* (2002), 4:279–87.

[7] The account I offer here, drawing on contemporary (non-Reformed) scholarship, is in its main thrust (i.e., the distinction between covenants of law and promise, as well as different "administrations" of the covenant of grace) already delineated at length in Francis Turretin's *Institutes of Elenctic Theology*, trans. George Musgrave Giger; ed. James T. Dennison, Jr., vol. 2: (Phillipsburg, NJ: Presbyterian and Reformed Publishing Company, 1993), Twelfth Topic (especially Qs. 4, 6, 7).

[8] Moshe Weinfeld, "The Covenant of Grant in the Old Testament and the Ancient Near East," *Journal of the American Oriental Society* 90 (1970), 185–86; cf. Suzanne Booer, *The Promise of the Land as an Oath* (Berlin: W. de Gruyter, 1992), for a more recent and extended treatment.

[9] Delbert R. Hillers, *Covenant: The History of a Biblical Idea* (Baltimore: Johns Hopkins University Press, 1969), 105. "A typical brief example runs as follows: 'From this day forward Niqmaddu son of Ammistamru king of Ugarit has taken the house of Pabeya [...] which is in Ullami, and given it to Nuriyana and to his descendants forever. Let no one take it from the hand of Nuriyana or his descendants forever. Seal of the king.'"

[10] G. E. Mendenhall, *Law and Covenant in Israel and the Ancient Near East* (Pittsburgh: The Biblical Colloquium, 1955), 37–38.

[11] Mendenhall, 38.

[12] Mendenhall, 39.

[13] E. P. Sanders, *Paul and Palestinian Judaism* (Minneapolis: Fortress, 1977); for "getting in by grace, staying in by obedience," see 93.178, 371, and for his definition of "covenantal nomism," see 75.543–556.

[14] Dennis McCarthy points out that "to cut a covenant" is used as early as the 1400s BCE in Aramaic and Phoenician as well as Hebrew records. From this ceremony is

derived the Hebrew idiom for making a treaty, *karat berith*, "to cut a treaty." Homer uses the same idiom: *horkia tamnein*, "to cut oaths" (55). See Dennis J. McCarthy, S. J., *Treaty and Covenant: A Study in the Ancient Oriental Documents and in the Old Testament* (Rome: Biblical Institute Press, 1963), 52–55.

[15] Mendenhall, 36.

[16] Hillers, 40–41.

[17] See Mendenhall, 45.

[18] Mendenhall, 46. Although Mendenhall perhaps speculates beyond the evidence on this point, it does remind us that while the two covenants were not intrinsically opposed (one pertained to the status of the nation, the other to the Davidic heir on the throne), they were not the same and tension could—and did—result between them in Israel's history. The love of the law is the goal of both covenants (Psalm 119 is consistent with Jeremiah 31); the difference is whether such love of the law and obedience to it function as a conditional basis or as the goal.

[19] Steven L. McKenzie, *Covenant* (St Louis: Chalice Press, 2000), 66. For seminal Davidic covenant passages, see 2 Sam. 7; 23:5; 1 Kings 8:15–26; 9:1–9; 15:4–5; 2 Kings 9:19; 1 Chron. 17; 22:12–13; 28:7–10; 2 Chron. 6:4–17; 7:12–22; 21:7; Ps. 89; 132; Jer. 33:14–26; Isa. 55:3.

[20] Mendenhall, 47.

[21] Mendenhall, 48.

[22] Mendenhall, 49.

[23] Jon D. Levenson, *Sinai and Zion: An Entry into the Jewish Bible* (San Francisco: HarperSanFrancisco, 1985), 24–25. Levenson offers a sound argument for Exodus 19:3b–8 being part of a source earlier than the Deuteronomic, reflecting "a relatively early phase in the religion of Israel" (25).

[24] Levenson, 31.

[25] Levenson, 33.

[26] Levenson, 34. It is worth noting that, with Dennis McCarthy, Mendenhall, and Hillers, among others, Levenson regards this material as pre-Penteteuchal and, in fact, "quite early" (35).

[27] Levenson, 75.

[28] Levenson, 78.

[29] In the book of Hebrews, the superiority of the new covenant is grounded not in the faithfulness of the Israelites but in God's eternal purpose and unilateral oath (6:13–20). The writer makes this point by tracing the path from the eternal covenant of redemption to the Abrahamic covenant and its Melchizedek priesthood (6:13–7:28) to the new covenant realized in Christ (chapters 8–10). All of this is contrasted with the old covenant throughout: a covenant that was temporary and conditional, and that is now obsolete (8:13).

[30] Levenson, 92.

[31] Levenson, 99.

[32] Levenson, 100.

[33] Levenson, 101.

[34] Levenson, 101.

[35] Levenson, 165.

[36] Levenson, 166.

[37] Levenson, 210.

[38] Levenson, 210.

[39] Levenson, 210.

[40] Levenson, 81.

[41] Levenson, 86.

[42] Levenson, 45.

[43] Levenson, 216. I would only add that in the New Testament, Sinai is not displaced but fulfilled. It is rendered obsolete not because it was wrong, but because it was always a temporary regime and reached its goal despite Israel's failures. In fact, precisely because Israel's representative servant has kept his Father's

word, even in this deeper (legal, not just typological) sense, the law-covenant has been fulfilled.

[44] Levenson, 194.

[45] Levenson, 209.

[46] For a representative summary of this very position among the seventeenth-century federal theologians, see Herman Witsius, *Economy of the Covenants* (1677) (reprinted from 1822 edition, Phillipsburg, NJ: P & R, 1990), book 2, chapter 2.

[47] Joseph Cardinal Ratzinger, *Many Religions—One Covenant: Israel, the Church and the World* (San Francisco: Ignatius Press, 1999), 36–47.

[48] Ratzinger, 36–47.

[49] Ratzinger, 50–51.

[50] Ratzinger, 55.

[51] Ratzinger, 56–57.

[52] Ratzinger, 64.

[53] Ratzinger, 66.

[54] Ratzinger, 67. However, the Reformers (certainly the covenant theology that arose in the Reformed tradition) did not contrast *covenant* with *testament*, as the writer suggests, but recognized that the specific type of *berith* of the Abrahamic- Davidic-new covenant was a promised inheritance (testament) rather than a mutual contract, and so could be served only by the Greek *diathēkē* rather than *synthēkē*. On this point, see Geerhardus Vos, "Hebrews: The Epistle of the Diatheke," *Princeton Theological Review* 13 (1915): 587–632 and 14 (1916):1–61, included in Richard B. Gaffin, Jr., ed., *Redemptive History and Biblical Interpretation: The Shorter Writings of Geerhardus Vos* (Phillipsburg, NJ: P & R, 1980), 161–233.

[55] Ratzinger, 67–68.

[56] Ratzinger, 67–68.

[57] Ratzinger, 68–71.

[58] Ratzinger, 62.

[59] Walter Brueggemann, *Theology of the Old Testament* (Minneapolis: Fortress, 1997), 419.

[60] Trevin Wax, "Interview with N. T. Wright—Responding to Piper on Justification," (13 Jan. 2009); http://trevinwax.com/2009/01/13/interview-with-nt-wright-responding-to-piper-on-justification/.

[61] Piper, *The Future of Justification: A Response to N. T. Wright* (Wheaton: Crossway, 2007), 37–38.

[62] Piper, 39.

[63] Piper, 45.

[64] Piper, 53; cf. 54–55.

[65] Wright, *What Saint Paul Really Said*, 98.

[66] Piper, 64–66.

[67] Piper, 68.

[68] Wright, *What Saint Paul Really Said*, 12.

[69] Piper, 64–68.

[70] Piper, 71.

[71] Piper, 79.

[72] Wright, *Paul: In Fresh Perspective*, 121. Piper also points out that Wright seems to use "according to" and "on the basis of" (works) as interchangeable (117–18).

[73] Wright, *What Saint Paul Really Said*, 129.

[74] N. T. Wright, "New Perspectives on Paul," in *Justification in Perspective: Historical Developments and Contemporary Challenges*, ed. Bruce L. McCormack (Baker Academic, 2006), 260.

[75] Wright, *Paul: In Fresh Perspective*, 148. As Piper points out, Wright's insistence

that justification is not the gospel and merely indicates a state of affairs rather than bringing about a new state of affairs seems to be contradicted by his statement in his commentary on *The Letter to the Romans*, 515: "Justification results in peace with God, in access to God's loving favor" (cited 98). Also, Wright underscores that although present justification is assurance of the state of things already in existence, future justification actually does create a new state of affairs, and it's on the basis of our works (Piper, 100; from Wright, "New Perspectives on Paul," 258). Therefore, "Wright's claim that 'the doctrine of justification by faith is not what Paul means by "the gospel"' and his claim that 'justification is not how someone becomes a Christian' are misleading." Wright calls this future assize "the final showdown," where God will finally condemn and save (101).

[76] Wright even says that "one of the great truths of the gospel" is "that the accomplishment of Jesus Christ is *reckoned* to all those who are 'in him.' This is the truth which has been expressed within the Reformed tradition in terms of 'imputed righteousness,' often stated in terms of Jesus Christ having fulfilled the moral law and thus having accumulated a 'righteous' status which can be shared with all his people. As with some other theological problems, I regard this as saying a substantially right thing in a substantially wrong way, and the trouble when you do that is that things on both sides of the equation, and the passages which are invoked to support them, become distorted....The mistake, as I see it, arises from the combination of the Reformers' proper sense of something being accomplished in Christ Jesus which is then reckoned to us, allied with their overemphasis on the category of *iustitia* as the catch-all, their consequent underemphasis on Paul's frequently repeated theology of our participation in the Messiah's death and resurrection, and their failure to locate Paul's soteriology itself on the larger map of God's plan for the whole creation. A proper re-emphasis on 'God's righteousness' as God's *own* righteousness should set all this straight." (quoted 122, from "Paul in Different Perspectives: Lecture 1"). Piper recognizes that Wright tends to merge "the imputation of a new position with the impartation of a new nature" (126). "But calling the present justification an anticipation of the 'final justification' while being ambiguous about the way our works function in the 'final justification' is not a strong way to assure us that present justification is not grounded in Spirit-enabled transformation" (129). Not only are faith and obedience necessarily connected. According to Wright, "Indeed, very often the word 'faith' itself could properly be translated as 'faithfulness,' which makes the point just as well" (*What Saint Paul Really Said*, 160). Piper nicely observes that racial boasting and self-help moralism are not radically different, as Wright maintains, but are expressions of self-righteousness (160).

[77] Piper provides this incisive comment by Simon Gathercole: "It is crucial to recognize that the New Perspective interpretation of [Romans] 4:1–8 falls to the

ground on this point: that David although circumcised, sabbatarian, and kosher, is described as without works because of his disobedience." Yet God counts righteousness to David (vv. 5, 8) (cited 169, from Simon J. Gathercole, *Where Is Boasting? Early Jewish Soteriology and Paul's Response in Romans 1–5* [Grand Rapids: Eerdmans, 2002], 247).

[78] Wax, "Interview with N. T. Wright—Responding to Piper on Justification."

CHAPTER 02

[1] As a Presbyterian, I will cite the Westminster standards, but the tendency is present in other Protestant confessions also.

[2] WCF 4:2, 6:6, 8:4, 15:2, 20:1, WSC 14, 40, 41, 83, WLC 17, 24, 39, 48, 91, 96, 97, 98, 150, 152, 153.

[3] Those who are interested will consult also the original Hebrew and Greek of 2 Chronicles 25:4, where the LXX translators did a similar thing.

[4] Douglas J. Moo, "'Law,' 'Works of the Law,' and Legalism in Paul," *Westminster Theological Journal* 45 (1983), 80.

[5] Op. cit., 88.

[6] James D. G. Dunn, "The New Perspective on Paul," *BJRL* 65 (August, 1982): 94–122. Reprinted in *Jesus, Paul and the Law,* (Louisville: John Knox, 1990). Cf. also Dunn's Galatians commentary and many of his other writings. The expression, "works of the law" appears in these passages: Rom. 3:20, 28; Gal. 2:16, 3:2, 5, and 10.

[7] The words "rely on" do not appear in the original. ESV's translation is very unfortunate here, not only because it is misleading but because it is contrary to its stated translation principle of "literal where possible." The KJV translates it literally, so it was/is possible to do so: "For as many as are of the works of the law are under the curse."

[8] I actually agree with Dunn's understanding of the problem at Galatia. Working independently of him, I had reached similar conclusions to his in my "The Problem at Galatia" (*Interpretation* 41 [January, 1987]: 32–43). The primary problem Paul addressed at Galatia was that insistence on observing the Mosaic Law necessarily

had the effect of continuing the ceremonial distinction between Jew and Gentile that was so much a part of that covenant, yet no part of the Christian covenant. Dunn is right in suggesting that, in the letter, the "marking" laws are especially odious to Paul; but Dunn is not convincing on the more-technical question of whether "works of the law" is only a reference to those marking laws.

[9] Jacob Neusner, *Judaism in the Beginning of Christianity* (Philadelphia: Fortress, 1984), 11–13.

[10] John Murray, *The Covenant of Grace: A Biblico-Theological Study* (London: Tyndale, 1954), 5.

[11] Murray, 14.

[12] For a fuller treatment of my disagreement with Murray regarding Galatians, cf. my "Abraham and Sinai Contrasted in Galatians 3:6–14" in *The Law is Not of Faith: Essays on Works and Grace in the Mosaic Covenant*, eds. Bryan Estelle, J. V. Fesko, and David VanDrunen (Phillipsburg, NJ: P&R, 2009), 240–58.

[13] *Redemptive History and Biblical Interpretation: The Shorter Writings of Geerhardus Vos*, ed. Richard B. Gaffin, Jr. (Phillipsburg, NJ: P&R, 2001), 15. Italics original.

[14] I discuss these matters in greater length in "Reflections on Auburn Theology," in *By Faith Alone*, eds. Gary L. W. Johnson and Guy P. Waters (Wheaton: Crossway, 2007), 113–25.

CHAPTER 03

[1] Brian Abel Ragen, *America* (29 January 1994).

[2] Harry Blamires, *A God Who Acts* (Ann Arbor, MI: Servant, 1979), 47.

[3] See Rachel Stahle, "The Guilt-Heavy Theology of Cotton Mather: Where Was God's Tender Mercy?" in *Modern Reformation* (November/December 1997).

[4] Keith Ward, *A Vision to Pursue: Beyond the Crisis in Christianity* (London: SCM, 1991).

[5] "The heart is deceitful above all things, and beyond cure" (Jer. 17:9).

CHAPTER 04

This essay was originally published as "Does Faith Mean Faithfulness?" in *Modern Reformation* 13, no. 4 (July/August 2004).

———————————

CHAPTER 05

[1] Jonathan Edwards, "Justification by Faith Alone," in *The Words of Jonathan Edwards: Vol. 19, Sermons and Discourses 1734–1738*, ed. M. X. Lesser (New Haven: Yale University Press, 2001), 215.

[2] Edwards, 22, 153.

[3] Edwards, 204.

[4] Edwards, 154.

[5] Edwards, 155.

[6] Edwards, 154.

[7] Edwards, 154.

[8] Edwards, 156.

[9] Edwards, 159.

[10] Francis Turretin, *Institutes of Elenctic Theology*, ed. James T. Dennison, Jr., trans. George Musgrave Giger, 3 vols. (Phillipsburg, NJ: Presbyterian and Reformed, 1994), 2:652.

[11] Turretin, 2:652.

[12] Turretin, 2:655, 674.

[13] Martin Luther, "Commentary on Psalm 51:8," in *Luther's Words*, ed. Jaroslav Pelikan (St. Louis: Concordia Publishing House, 1955).

[14] Paul Althaus, *The Theology of Martin Luther* (Philadelphia: Fortress Press, 1966).

[15] Luther, 164.

[16] Luther, 167.

[17] John Calvin, *Institutes of the Christian Religion*, ed. John T. McNeill, trans. Ford Lewis Battles (Philadelphia: Westminster Press, 1960), 3.11.10.

[18] Calvin, 3.16.1.

[19] Edwards, 155.

[20] Edwards, 156.

[21] Edwards, 158.

[22] Edwards, 147.

This essay was originally published as "The Nature of Justifying Faith" in *Modern Reformation* 16, no. 5 (September/October 2007).

CHAPTER 07

[1] See *Christianity Today* (8 December 1997), 35–8.

[2] Timothy George, Thomas C. Oden, and J. I. Packer, "An Open Letter About 'The Gift of Salvation,'" *Christianity Today* (27 April 1998), 9.

[3] George, Oden, and Packer, 9.

This essay was originally published as "Not by Faith Alone: The Roman Catholic Doctrine of Justification: An Interview with Robert Sungenis" in *Modern Reformation* 16, no. 5 (September/October 2007).

CHAPTER 08

This essay was originally published as "What 'Evangelicals and Catholics Together' Ignores: The Inseparable Link between Imputation and the Gospel" in *Modern Reformation* 7, no. 5 (September/October 1998).

CHAPTER 09

"Ten Propositions on Faith and Salvation" was originally published in *Christ the Lord: The Reformation and Lordship Salvation*, ed. Michael Horton (Grand Rapids: Baker, 1995), 209–10.

CHAPTER 10

[1] Louis Berkhof, *Systematic Theology: New Combined Edition* (1932–38; Grand Rapids: Eerdmans, 1996), 449.

[2] A. A. Hodge, *Outlines of Theology* (1879; Edinburgh: Banner of Truth, 1991), 483.

[3] See, for example, Albert Schweitzer, *The Mysticism of Paul the Apostle* (1931; Baltimore: Johns Hopkins UP, 1998), 223; and Albrecht Ritschl, *The Christian Doctrine of Justification and Reconciliation* (1902; Eugene: Wipf and Stock, 2004), 94.

[4] See Travis Tamerius, "Interview with N. T. Wright," *Reformation and Revival*, 11/1 (2002), 129; N. T. Wright, "New Perspectives on Paul," in *Justification in Perspective: Historical Developments and Contemporary Challenges*, ed. Bruce L. McCormack (Grand Rapids: Baker, 2006), 255–56; A. T. B. McGowan, "Justification and the Ordo Salutis," in *Justification in Perspective: Historical Developments and Contemporary Challenges*, ed. Bruce McCormack (Grand Rapids: Baker, 2006), 156–57; and Richard B. Gaffin, "Union with Christ: Some Biblical and Theological Reflections," in *Always Reforming: Explorations in Systematic Theology*, ed. A. T. B. McGowan (Leicester: Apollos, 2006), 275.

[5] Rich Lusk, "Private Communication 27 May 2003," cited in James B. Jordan, "Merit vs. Maturity: What Did Jesus Do for Us?" in *The Federal Vision*, eds. Steve Wilkins and Duane Garner (Monroe: Athanasius Press, 2004), 155.

[6] Rich Lusk, "A Response to 'The Biblical Plan of Salvation,'" in *The Auburn Avenue Theology: Pros and Cons. Debating the Federal Vision*, ed. E. Calvin Beisner (Ft. Lauderdale: Knox Theological Seminary, 2004), 42.

[7] John Murray, *The Imputation of Adam's Sin* (Phillipsburg: P and R, 1959), 76

[8] Hodge, *Outlines of Theology*, 482.

[9] Berkhof, *Systematic Theology*, 452.

This essay was originally published as "The Doctrine of Justification: The Article on Which the Church Stands or Falls" in *Modern Reformation* 11, no. 2 (March/April 2002).

CHAPTER 11

This essay was originally published as "A More Perfect Union? Justification and Union with Christ" in *Modern Reformation* 17, no. 3 (May/June 2007).

CHAPTER 12

[1] See Dennis E. Tamburello, "Dominus Iesus: A Stumbling Block to Reformed-Catholic Dialogue?" in *Concord Makes Strength: Essays in Reformed Ecumenism*, ed. John W. Coakley (Grand Rapids: William B. Eerdmans, 2002), 77–87.

[2] *Institutes* 1.2.1. Translations of the *Institutes* are taken from *Institutes of the Christian Religion*, ed. John T. McNeill, trans. Ford Lewis Battles, Library of Christian Classics, vols. 20 and 21 (Philadelphia: Westminster Press, 1960).

[3] *Institutes* 1.2.2.

[4] For example, a Calvin volume was recently added to Paulist Press's Classics of Western Spirituality series: *John Calvin: Writings on Pastoral Piety*, ed. Elsie Anne McKee (New York: Paulist, 2002).

[5] *Institutes* 3.2.25.

[6] Anna Case-Winters, "Joint Declaration on Justification: Reformed Comments," in *Concord Makes Strength*, 91–92.

[7] David and Thomas Torrance, eds., *Calvin's New Testament Commentaries,* vol. 11, *Galatians, Ephesians, Philippians, and Colossians*, trans. T. H. L. Parker (Grand Rapids: Eerdmans, 1965), 43. For a more complete treatment of this topic, see my *Union with Christ: John Calvin and the Mysticism of St. Bernard*, Columbia Series in Reformed Theology (Louisville: Westminster John Knox Press, 1994), 86–87, 100–01.

[8] "The Presence of Christ in Church and World," in *Growth in Agreement: Reports*

and Agreed Statements of Ecumenical Conversations on a World Level, eds. Harding Meyer and Lukas Vischer (New York: Paulist Press, 1984), 456.

[9] See especially *Institutes* 4.17.16 and 4.17.33.

[10] See the *Catechism of the Catholic Church* (United States Catholic Conference, Inc.-Libreria Editrice Vaticana, 1994), par. 1397.

[11] *Institutes* 4.17.38.

[12] *Institutes* 4.17.44.

[13] *Institutes* 4.17.46 (emphasis added).

[14] *Institutes* 3.2.7.

[15] *Institutes* 3.1.3.

[16] *Institutes* 4.17.33.

[17] Friedrich Schleiermacher, *The Christian Faith,* eds. H. R. Mackintosh and J. S. Steward (Philadelphia: Fortress Press, 1976), 574.

[18] "Presence of Christ in Church and World," 445.

[19] J. K. S. Reid, ed., *Calvin: Theological Treatises,* Library of Christian Classics, vol. 22 (Philadelphia: Westminster Press, 1954), 228.

[20] *Institutes* 1.2.1.

[21] Calvin makes this point with particular clarity in his commentary on Galatians 5:14, where he describes love of neighbor as proof of our love of God. *Calvin's New Testament Commentaries,* vol. 11, 100–01. See also B. A. Gerrish's excellent study, *Grace and Gratitude: The Eucharistic Theology of John Calvin* (Minneapolis: Fortress Press, 1993).

[22] This essay was originally published as "Justification and Sanctification Distinguished" in *Modern Reformation* 11, no. 2 (March/April 2002).

NOTES

CHAPTER 13

This abridged essay is reprinted by kind permission of Fr. Tamburello and the Institute for Reformed Theology. It was first published in *The Bulletin of the Institute for Reformed Theology* (Winter 2004, vol. 4, no. 1). This essay was also published as "Christ at the Center: The Legacy of the Reformed Tradition" in *Modern Reformation* 18, no. 7 (Special Issue 2009).

CHAPTER 14

This essay was originally published as "The Discomfort of the Justified Life" in *Modern Reformation* 15, no. 4 (July/August 2006).

CHAPTER 15

[1] Carter Lindberg, *The Third Reformation?: Charismatic Movements and the Lutheran Tradition* (Macon, GA: Mercer University Press, 1983), 180.

[2] David Scaer, "Sanctification in Lutheran Theology," *Concordia Theological Quarterly*, 49:2, 3, 188.

[3] Martin Luther, *AE* 34, 111.

[4] I am indebted to Robert Kolb (Concordia Seminary, St. Louis) for his summary of this and many other aspects of Luther's "Theology of the Cross."

This essay was originally published as "Finding True Peace with God" in *Modern Reformation* 11, no. 2 (March/April 2002).

CHAPTER 16

This essay was originally published as "Holiness: God's Work or Ours?" in *Modern Reformation* 5, no. 6 (November/December 1996).

CHAPTER 17

This essay was originally published as "Holiness Wars: The Antinomianism Debate" in *Modern Reformation* 21, no. 6 (November/December 2012).

CONCLUSION

[1] See Michael Horton, "What's All the Fuss About? The Status of the Justification Debate," *Modern Reformation* 11, no. 2 (March/April 2002), 17–21.

[2] Charles G. Finney, *Systematic Theology* (Minneapolis: Bethany, 1976), 320.

[3] Charles G. Finney, *Revivals of Religion* (Old Tappan, NJ: Revell, n.d.), 4–5.

[4] Finney, *Revivals of Religion*, 321. Italics in the original.

[5] See Keith J. Hardman, *Charles Grandison Finney: Revivalist and Reformer* (Grand Rapids, Baker, 1990), 380–94.

[6] See, for example, Whitney R. Cross, *The Burned-Over District: The Social and Intellectual History of Enthusiastic Religion in Western New York, 1800–1850* (Ithaca, NY: Cornell University Press, 1982).

[7] Dietrich Bonhoeffer, "Protestantism without the Reformation," in *No Rusty Swords: Letters, Lectures and Notes, 1928–1936*, ed. Edwin H. Robertson, trans. Edwin H. Robertson and John Bowden (London: Collins, 1965), 92–118.

[8] William H. Willimon, *The Intrusive Word: Preaching to the Unbaptized* (Eugene, OR: Wipf & Stock, 2002), 53.

[9] Willimon, 20.

[10] Willimon, 21, citing George Barna, *Marketing the Church: What They Never Taught You about Church Growth* (Colorado Springs: NavPress, 1988), 50.

[11] Willimon, 38.

[12] Willimon, 43.

[13] Willimon, 52.

[14] George Lindbeck, "Justification and Atonement: An Ecumenical Trajectory," in Joseph A. Burgess and Marc Kolden, eds., *By Faith Alone: Essays on Justification in Honor of Gerhard O. Forde* (Grand Rapids: Eerdmans, 2004), 205.

[15] Lindbeck, 207.

[16] Lindbeck, 207–08.

[17] Lindbeck, 209.

[18] Lindbeck, 211.

[19] G. C. Berkouwer, *Studies in Dogmatics: Faith and Sanctification* (Grand Rapids: Eerdmans, 1952), 11–12.

[20] Stanley Grenz, *Revisioning Evangelical Theology: A Fresh Agenda for the 21 Century* (Downers Grove, IL: IVP, 1993), 17, 31, and throughout the volume.

[21] Grenz, 30, 34.

[22] Grenz, 32.

[23] Grenz, 33.

[24] Grenz, 38, 41.

[25] Grenz, 41–42.

[26] Grenz, 44.

[27] Grenz, 45.

[28] Grenz, 46.

[29] Grenz, 48.

[30] Grenz, 52.

[31] Grenz, 54.

[32] Grenz, 55.

NOTES

[33] Grenz, 62.

[34] Martin Luther, *Lectures on Galatians 1535,* vol. 26, *Luther's Works,* eds. Jaroslav Pelikan and Walter A. Hansen (St. Louis, MO: Concordia Publishing House, 1963), 132.

[35] John Calvin, *Institutes of the Christian Religion,* 3.19.5.

[36] William Ames, *Marrow of Theology* (Grand Rapids: Baker Academic, 1997), 171.

[37] Berkouwer, 93.

[38] Berkouwer, 77–78.

[39] Berkouwer, 20.

[40] Cited in Berkouwer, 22.

[41] Berkouwer, 20.

JERRY BRIDGES is an author and conference speaker. He has been on the staff of The Navigators for over fifty years and currently serves on the Collegiate Mission.

JOHN V. FESKO is academic dean and professor of systematic theology and historical theology at Westminster Seminary California in Escondido, California.

SIMON GATHERCOLE is lecturer in New Testament studies and fellow at Fitzwilliam College, University of Cambridge, United Kingdom.

RYAN GLOMSRUD is associate professor of historical theology at Westminster Seminary California and executive editor of *Modern Reformation* magazine.

W. ROBERT GODFREY is professor of church history and president of Westminster Seminary California.

T. DAVID GORDON is a minister in the Presbyterian Church in America and associate professor of religion at Grove City College in Grove City, Pennsylvania.

MICHAEL S. HORTON is the J. Gresham Machen Professor of Systematic Theology and Apologetics at Westminster Seminary California, host of *White Horse Inn* national radio broadcast, and editor-in-chief of *Modern Reformation* magazine.

GEORGE HUNSINGER is the Hazel Thompson McCord Professor of Systematic Theology at Princeton Theological Seminary.

KEN JONES is pastor of Glendale Missionary Baptist Church in Miami, Florida, and a cohost of *White Horse Inn* radio program.

J. A. O. PREUS III is executive vice president for Mission Advancement for Bethesda Lutheran Communities in Watertown, Wisconsin.

HAROLD L. SENKBEIL is executive director for spiritual care with Doxology, the Lutheran Center for Spiritual Care and Counsel.

R.C. SPROUL is the founder and chairman of Ligonier Ministries in Orlando, Florida.

DENNIS E. TAMBURELLO, OFM, is professor of religious studies at Siena College in Loudonville, New York.

DAVID VANDRUNEN is the Robert B. Strimple Professor of Systematic Theology and Christian Ethics at Westminster Seminary California in Escondido, California.

MP3 CD CONTENT

1. You Foolish Galatians!

2. Understanding the Indicative & the Imperative

3. Getting Back to Basics

4. Romans 3–4: Sin, Righteousness & Justification

5. Romans 5: Justification & Reconciliation

6. Faith Alone

7. Understanding Imputation

8. Jesus, James & Paul

9. Dealing with Difficult Verses

10. Current Controversies over Justification

11. Roman Catholics & Justification

12. The Theology of N. T. Wright

13. The Heart of Christianity

14. A Survey of Christian Faith & Practice

15. Should We Reform or Abandon American Protestantism?

16. What Still Divides Us? The Catholic View of Justification

17. What Still Divides Us? The Protestant View of Justification

18. What Still Divides Us? Cross Examination

19. .epub file of *Justified*

20. Pdf of WHI show descriptions

Made in the USA
Charleston, SC
16 May 2013